THE GUINNESS
BOOK OF

CRICKET
EXTRAS

David Rayvern Allen

GUINNESS BOOKS

Editor: Honor Head
Design and Layout: Michael Morey

© David Rayvern Allen and Guinness Publishing Ltd, 1988

Published in Great Britain by Guinness Publishing Ltd,
33 London Road, Enfield, Middlesex

Typeset in Meridien
by Ace Filmsetting Ltd, Frome, Somerset
Printed and bound in Great Britain by The Bath Press, Bath

'Guinness' is a registered trade mark of Guinness Superlatives Ltd

British Library Cataloguing in Publication Data
Allen, David Rayvern
    Cricket extras.
    1. Cricket
    I. Title
    796.35′8
    ISBN 0-85112-485-2

After cricket, David Rayvern Allen's second hobby is music. His interest in the weird and wonderful in both probably stems from his off-beat cymbal playing during National Service days. He then played on-beat piano in theatres and recital rooms before progressing to television to work on programmes ranging from opera to variety. Since then, he has worked as a producer for all the networks on BBC Radio, a demanding career which has not stopped him writing a diverse selection of books including *A Song for Cricket*, a biography of Sir Charles Aubrey Smith, several anthologies of John Arlott's broadcasts and writings, and *The Punch Book of Cricket*, as well as contributing to *Barclay's World of Cricket*, *The Cricketer* and *Wisden's Cricket Monthly*.

Likewise, David's prolific writing has not prevented him from winning a number of awards as a producer, including an Ivor Novello Award and the Best European Light Entertainment Programme Prize at Monaco in 1983.

David says his favourite sport is tiddlywinks, but as yet has not found anyone willing to publish the book or broadcast the programme . . .

Thanks to those who, in various ways, have assisted considerably in putting together *Cricket Extras*: Honor Head, Bunty Ireland, David Frith, Gerald Brodribb, Benny Green, Marcus Williams, Tony Lewis and Stephen Green.

CONTENTS

A HISTORETTE OF CRICKET 6

PLAYING THE GAME 10

LONG HITS *10* / BOUNDARIES GALORE AND GLORIOUS BATTING *12* / BOWLED OVER *17* / CAUGHT OUT *20* / THROWING THE BALL *23* / EXTRAS EXTRAS *23* / BAIL AWAY *25* / HOWZAT! *27* / CRICKET DRESS *30*

A CLASS APART 32

CRICKET AND ROYALTY *32* / CRICKETING ARISTOCRATS *35*

A SECOND CHILDHOOD 38

SENIOR CITIZENS *38* / JUNIOR MEMBERS *40*

WHAT'S IN A NAME 41

NICKNAMES *41* / STRANGERS IN THE CAMP *43* / OPPOSING SIDES *44* / FAMILY TEAMS *47*

AWAY FROM THE GAME 48

EARNING A CRUST *48* / OFF-PITCH ACHIEVEMENTS *50*

A BAT A BRIEF AND MORE 54

CRICKET AND THE LAW *56* / CRICKET IN DISPUTE *61*

CRICKET'S CASUALTIES 64

ON THE FIELD *64* / OFF THE FIELD *67* / THE CASUALTIES WHO ROSE FROM THE DEAD *70*

CRICKET GETS CURIOSER AND CURIOSER 71

EXTRAORDINARY OCCURENCES *71* / ODD FACTS AND FEATS *78* / GAMES IN UNUSUAL AND DIFFICULT CIRCUMSTANCES *85*

THE SPOKEN WORD 87
TALES WITH TAGS 87 / QUOTES 91

GOING, GOING, GONE . . . 94

CRICKET AND THE PUB 95

CRICKET AND CREATURES GREAT AND SMALL 97
FROM CAT TO RAT 97 / BOWLED OVER BIRDS 100 / INSECT INCIDENCE 100 / SHORT SHARK SHOCK 101

CRICKET AND THE CHURCH 102

WOMEN AND CRICKET 107

LITERARY LINKS 114

THE ROAR OF THE GREASEPAINT, THE SMELL OF THE CROWD 117
MUSIC 117 / CRICKETERS WHO ALSO PLAYED . . . 119 / MUSICIANS WHO ALSO PLAYED . . . 120 / CRICKETING SONGS 121 / MEDIA 121 / THE STAGE 122

BIBLIOGRAPHY 128

A HISTORETTE OF CRICKET

In the beginning there was the sward and on it shepherds watched their flocks by day; or they should have done. Instead, they carved bats from wood, made balls from wool, and then threw them at a handy tree stump. Lo and behold! – a game was born.

This happened in the Weald in times since described as Dark, which one would think has absolutely nothing to do with a pyjama pastime, surrounded by razzmatazz and hype, that has been played under stadium floodlights on the other side of the world.

But the one game begat the other, even if it did take 700 years, and was not always called cricket.

The first generally accepted reference to a fundamental form of bat and ball is found in the wardrobe accounts of King Edward I. In 1300, he 'shelled out' six quid for his son's cricketing gear which shows that, even in those days, royal equipment was not cheap.

After that touch of monarchical munificence, the next 400 years or so took cover under fairly heavy cumulus with periodic shafts of light revealing such things as reprisals for playing cricket on Sundays, a court case over disputed land on which games had taken place, its inclusion in sports proscribed by Cromwell's Commissioners and English expatriates knocking a ball about in the Middle East.

Then in 1706, a certain William Goldwin, one time Headmaster of Bristol Grammar School, produced the first full description of a match in Latin. Subsequently, events occurred with a regularity more discernible.

1709 First known county match: Kent v Surrey at Dartford.

1725 First recorded match on the Artillery ground, Finsbury. Cricket is still being played on the HAC Ground off the City Road.

1727 Articles of agreement regarding the conduct of matches between teams led by the second Duke of Richmond and Mr Brodrick of Peperharow. First such extant. Probably there were earlier articles of agreement.

1729 Date of earliest surviving bat: inscribed 'J.C. 1729'. John Chitty's bat is kept in the Oval Pavilion.

1741 Cricket played on Christmas Day at Savannah, Georgia, USA.

1744 June 18. First really important match of which the full score has been preserved: Kent v All England. Kent won by 1 wicket and James Dance, alias Love, furnished a vivid description in his *Cricket: a Heroic Poem* published this same year. A less important match whose score survives was played a little time before the above encounter.
First known issue of the *Laws of Cricket*: a recension of an earlier code.
First recorded charge for admission: 2d to the Artillery Ground.

c 1750 Foundation of the Hambledon Club: they played first on Broadhalfpenny and then Windmill Down. Some historians give a later date for the formation.

1751 A match in New York between New York and a London XI 'played according to the London method'.

1769 The first recorded century.

John Minshull scored 107 for Duke of Dorset's XI v Wrotham.

1776 Earliest known score-cards, printed by T Pratt, scorer to the Vine Club, Sevenoaks.

1787 Cricket begins at Thomas Lord's first ground, Dorset Square. The MCC, as such, is formed.

1789 The first English tour abroad, to Paris, is aborted at Dover owing to the French Revolution. Cricketers prefer to keep their heads.

1790/1 The first publication of match scores, by Samuel Britcher. Possibly there were earlier offerings that have not survived. Cricket was now one of around 400 published works on all subjects issued yearly.

1796 A match between Eton and Westminster at Hounslow. The encounter was played in defiance of the Headmaster of Eton, Dr Heath, who flogged the whole eleven on their return. It must have been a painful day as they lost by 66 runs.

1800/1 Thomas Boxall gave his name to the first instructional book on cricket in English.

1806 Reference to a meeting of St Anne's Cricket Club in Barbados – first such known of West Indian cricket. Recently found belt buckle depicting the game in the Caribbean probably *c* mid-18th century.

1809 Lord's second ground opened at North Bank, subsequently bisected by the construction of the Regent Canal.

1814 Lord's third ground opened on its present site. The turf was transferred on each move.

1820 First recorded individual score of over 200. William Ward made 278 for MCC v Norfolk at Lord's.

1822 John Willes is 'no-balled' for throwing; in other words, bowling round-arm.

1828 Bowlers are now allowed to raise their arm level with their elbow due to an amendment in the law.

1833 Nyren's *The Young Cricketers Tutor* and *The Cricketers of My Time* compiled by Charles Cowden Clarke is published. An invaluable depiction of late 18th century cricket.

1837 F W Lillywhite took 120 wickets in important matches, the first time 100 had been captured.

1838 Opening of Trent Bridge ground, Nottingham, by William Clarke.

1845 W Hillyer took 208 wickets in important matches, the first time 200 had been captured.
The first match at Kennington Oval.

1846 Clarke's 'All England XI' began playing matches all over the country, thereby performing missionary work in some remote areas.
Score-cards first sold at Lord's.

1848 W G Grace born on July 18.

1849 First match between Yorkshire and Lancashire.

c 1850 Mowing machine used for first time on cricket grounds. Sheep continued to do the job at Lord's.

c 1850 First inter-colonial match, Tasmania v Victoria at Launceston.

1851 Hong Kong CC formed.

1852 The United All England XI constituted in rivalry to Clarke's lot. In later years the United North of England and United South of England XIs sprang up.

1855 William Clarke takes 476 wickets in a season, an extraordinary total.

1858 The first recorded instance of a hat being given to a bowler for taking three wickets with consecutive balls.

1859 First touring party leaves for Canada and the USA with George Parr captaining an English team.

1861/2 First visit of an English side to Australia under H H Stephenson.

1862 Edgar Willsher 'no-balled' for having his hand higher than his shoulder in a match between England and Surrey at the Oval.

1864 Overarm bowling legalized. First issue of *Wisden's Cricketers' Almanack*.

1868 Visit to England of Australian Aborigine team.

1870 Heavy roller first used at Lord's.

1873 W G Grace the first to do the double (1,000 runs, 100 wickets) in first-class cricket.

1874 An American baseball side beat MCC at cricket in a match at Lord's.

1878 Australian side visit England for first time.

1879 A team from New Zealand undertake a tour for the first time: Canterbury to Victoria and Tasmania.

1880 First Test Match in England: England beat Australia by 5 wickets.

1882 Tradition of 'The Ashes' established after obituary notice to English cricket published in the *Sporting Times*. Australia had beaten England by 7 runs at the Oval and a spectator had become so excited that he had a heart attack and died.

1886 Parsee team visits England.

1888 C T B Turner took 283 wickets in first-class matches during the Australian tour of England, a total not reached by any other overseas cricketer.

1888/9 First tour by English side to South Africa.

1892 The first Dutch team toured England: the Gentlemen of Holland. The tea interval is first mentioned in a match between Scotland and Yorkshire at Glasgow.

1894 First visit of South African team to England.

1894/5 The word 'Test' first used by *Pall Mall Gazette*.

1895 First visit by an English team to the West Indies.

1895 W G Grace scores his hundredth hundred.

By the 1890s cricket had come of age. A County Championship had been established. Visits to and from other countries had become expected. And powerful personalities such as Grace, Ranji, MacLaren and Spofforth dominated cricketing arenas and newspaper headlines. Throughout the 19th century and even earlier, disciples of the gospel had fingered every page of the atlas. Aside from the Empire, practitioners had pitched stumps in unlikely venues; a choice trio are the Spitzbergen ice-cap, a bridge over the Bosphorus and a battlefield near Mons. The game had also attracted the attention of a memoir-writing Swiss gentleman, inspired a treatise in Spanish to be published in Buenos Aires and encouraged a non-violent encounter in Cape Province between Hottentots and Afrikaner Boers that was won by the former. Without too many exceptions, the spread worldwide had been hand-in-glove with British imperialist rule.

In England itself, cricket reflected the glow of the late Victorian and Edwardian eras, gloried in the strokes of Jessop, Fry and Gunn, admired Trumper's artistry and then took a more chastened and cynical view at the end of the First World War. Wanting to forget that watershed, public imagination was soon rekindled with the feats of not only old but new heroes: Hobbs, Hendren, Hammond, Macartney, Mailey and, of course, Bradman. Then came 'Bodyline', the televising of a Test in 1938 and a flying bomb over Lord's during a match in 1944.

The second post-war era saw another re-awakening. Compton and Edrich rewriting the record book in 1947, the all-conquering Aussies in '48, the brilliant West Indies side of 1950 containing the three Ws, Ramadhin and Valentine, England's recapture of 'the Ashes' in '53, Surrey's incredible sequence of championship success and the transition during the 1960s to the irresistible pull of market forces which led to the one-day limited-over formula and a decade later, the Packer revolution. Concurrent with such radical change, cricket has continued to stagger through a political minefield triggered in 1968 by the D'Oliveira issue and also tried to keep its ideals and manners in a world of considerable upheaval, where it has had to contend with a number of social habitudes that are distinctly unappealing. Often there appears to be an armoured car instead of a breathless hush in the close. Will the game survive? It must.

PLAYING THE GAME

LONG HITS

There are few aspects of cricket more likely to arouse the enthusiasm of spectators than to see a batsman lofting a ball over the boundary yet, at the same time, it is almost impossible to calculate accurately a mighty stroke that could have cleared the heads of spectators and fallen to ground out of sight and away from immediate access. Therefore, nobody can really be dogmatic over respective distances:

In 1856, Walter Fellows, while practising on the Christchurch Ground at Oxford, is reported to have driven a ball 175 yds from hit to pitch. Many have found this distance hard to accept.

J E C Moore had a measured hit of 170 yds 1 ft 5 in in a minor match at Griffith, NSW 1930.

That magnificent smiter C I 'Buns' Thornton is supposed to have once struck a ball 168 yds 2 ft at Brighton. Thornton himself only claimed 162 yds.

V F S Crawford, of Surrey and Leicestershire, whose initials earned him the sobriquet 'very fast scorer', in 1900 drove a ball over the pavilion at Bristol and out of the ground – a measured 160 yds.

W H Fowler had a hit of 157 yds checked during the MCC v Somerset match at Lord's in 1882.

Albert Trott, playing for MCC v Australians at Lord's in 1899 hit a ball from M A Noble over the pavilion, the only time such a feat has been achieved. Trott made a potentially even bigger hit a few weeks earlier, when he hoisted a ball from Fred Tate, which struck an 'MCC emblem' on the pinnacle of the pavilion and rebounded back.

At Wanganui, during the 1882/3 season, C Cox struck a ball 156 yds, maybe the longest hit in New Zealand. A few years later W J Ford of Middlesex smote a ball 'far out of the ground into the sea' at Nelson and nobody was able to estimate the distance.

A batsman called Hemmings playing for the famous Brighton Brunswick Club hit a ball through a window of a dining-room of one of the houses overlooking the ground. The owner of the house refused to return the ball until the value of the window had been handed over.

Garfield Sobers, playing for South Australia against Queensland at Brisbane, struck a six which bounced off the roof of the Sir Leslie Wilson pavilion and finally reached the forecourt of a garage 60 or so yards outside the ground.

In 1900, G L Jessop hit a ball which landed on the North turret of the pavilion at Lord's and just failed to go right over.

Doug Walters, when 16 years of age and playing for NSW Colts, hit a ball out of Sydney Cricket Ground into Kippaxhake, a distance of some 150 yds.

A member of the Melbourne CC offered a reward to anyone who could hit the ball against the clock on top of the pavilion. That colossal smiter G F Bonnor collected the reward after he struck the clock face and broke it.

Professor Gerald Brodribb, who perhaps knows more about long hits than any other person, tells the story in his book *Hit for Six* of how, at Bradford in 1914, Jack Hobbs hit a ball from Alonzo Drake of Yorkshire on to the face of the clock on the football stand. The time of the strike was 4 o'clock, both for Hobbs and the clock. The wounded minute-hand inched on valiantly for a further ten minutes before expiring with a flop to rest in peace above the figure 6 with the time showing half-past four. In fact, the hand rested in war as well because it was not repaired until after hostilities had ceased four years later. At the time, however, the disgruntled Drake, who had taken a pasting from Hobbs remarked that 't'was a pity 'ands 'adn't been knocked t'six-

thirty as then we'd 'ave been
finished with this mucking abaht
for t'day'.

BOUNDARIES GALORE
AND GLORIOUS BATTING

Greville Stevens holds the record for
the most boundaries known in any
class of cricket. In an inter-house
game at University College School
in 1919, he hit 24 sixes and 64 fours
during his innings of 466 not out.
Nearly 250 of Stevens' runs came in
a ninth-wicket stand and in the
total of 548 the rest of the side only
managed to accumulate 38. Extras
accounted for 44. Stevens also took
13 wickets and 4 catches in the
match.

Percy Perrin scored 272 of his 343
not out with 68 fours when batting
for Essex against Derbyshire at
Queen's Park, Chesterfield in 1904 –
the most boundaries on record in
any first-class innings.

George Arcadiou, the son of a Greek
panel-beater, scored 425 including
58 fours in 470 minutes for Druids v
North Sunshine in a Melbourne
junior game when aged 16, 1967/8.

A batsman called Hope hit 36 sixes
in a single innings in a club game at
Durban, South Africa in December
1939. Apparently, the match was
not for *charity*.

G Ivanoff, obviously of Eastern
European extraction, hit 11 sixes in
successive scoring strokes for
Pymble v Berowra at Sydney, 1967.
   In a match at the Alamein Club,
Cairo, between a South African XI
and Military Police in 1942, the

renowned Dudley Nourse hit 9
successive balls for six and then
eventually struck 11 sixes in 12
balls.

That colossal striker, 'Jim' Smith hit
nine sixes off successive balls in
1935 for a Middlesex XI against
Harrow and District at Rayner's
Lane.

Ian Botham hit 80 sixes in first-class
and one-day matches in 1985 – a
record for a season.

The record amount of runs off one
over in first-class cricket was set by
Garfield Sobers when he hit 6 sixes
off the bowling of Malcolm Nash
when playing for Nottinghamshire
against Glamorgan at Swansea in
1968. This feat was equalled by Ravi
Shastri in 1985 for Bombay against
Baroda.

W J Stewart, playing for
Warwickshire v Lancashire at
Blackpool in 1985 hit 17 sixes; 10 in
a first innings of 155 and 7 in his
second innings of 125.

The unlikely total of 286 has been
scored from a single hit. A team
from Victoria was playing another
from Bunbury in Western Australia
and the first ball of the match was
hit into 'a three-pronged branch of a
tall Jarrah tree'. As runs started to
accumulate in alarming fashion, the
fielding side claimed 'lost ball'. 'Not
so,' said the Umpire, 'we can all see
it.' An axe to saw off a branch could
not be found, so eventually someone
produced a rifle and after a number
of attempts thwarted by poor
marksmanship and with
ammunition running low, the ball
was shot to the ground. The

exhausted batsmen collapsed in a heap having run in excess of three and a half miles.

A batsman called George Hemingway once ran 250 while the fielders argued as to who should retrieve the ball from a bed of nettles.

It has been reported that a hit for 67 was once made at the Beacon Hill ground at Rottingdean in Sussex. Unsurprisingly, a lofted drive ran down the hill into the village, from where the ball was returned by a fielding relay. The fielder near the summit of the hill, however, in his enthusiasm overthrew, with the result that the ball ran away down the other side of the hill. Retrieving the ball was redolent of crazy golf.

37 runs was once scored from a single hit, in a village game, the pitch being at the top of a hill and down which the ball was hit. A relay of fielders helped to return it to the wicket-keeper.

F P Miller scored 13 off one stroke at single wicket, again assisted by a

slope. When returning the ball the exhausted fielder had to keep chasing his own throws uphill.

A N Hornby scored 10 from a single hit at the Oval in 1873 when playing for Lancashire against Surrey. The feat was repeated north of the Thames in 1900 by Samuel Wood when appearing for Derbyshire against the MCC at Lord's.

J H T Roupell made 97 for Trinity Hall against Emmanuel College at Cambridge in 1865. In his score was a 10, a 9, an 8 – all without overthrows. The hit for 10 travelled a distance of some 240 yds.

In 1890, B D Gagrat ran 9 for a hit to leg in a match at Bombay.

Paul Pittioni scored possibly the fastest century of all time in an organized match when at the age of 13, in March 1982, he reached a hundred in 16 minutes for St Patrick's Marist Brothers High School, Dundas v Epping YMCA.

Percy Fender scored the fastest first-class hundred for Surrey against Northampton at Northampton in 1920 in 35 minutes. Steve O'Shaughnessy equalled the time 63 years later in a game between Lancashire and Leicestershire at Old Trafford. There the comparison ends, as O'Shaughnessy was being fed full tosses and long-hops by two non-bowlers in the hope of expediting a declaration.

Don Bradman scored a remarkable century off only 22 balls in 3 overs

consisting of 8 balls each. This happened at Blackheath, NSW in 1931 in a local match to test an experimental surface.

Laurie Quinlan, playing for Trinity against Mercantile in 1910 scored a century in 18 minutes. This time was equalled by Russell Penny during the 1985/6 season.

Peter Heine, South African fast bowler, crashed 123 not out in 22 minutes in a senior club game in Pretoria, 1950–51.

When W N Roe batted for Emmanuel against Caius in 1881 he saw that the scorers had given him 415 runs, not out. He went over and told them that he had been counting and that his actual score was 416.

W Hyman of Somerset, playing for Bath Association, scored 359 not out in a total of 461 for six achieved in 100 minutes. Hyman hit E M Grace, bowling for Thornbury, for 62 in two consecutive overs. His innings contained 32 sixes and with T Taylor (44 not out) added 259 in three-quarters of an hour.

In 1882, in a match at Moradabad between two companies of the 51st Regiment, Private Davis made 50 in eight hits – an 8, a 7, five 6s and one 5.

'Shunter' Coen, South African Test batsman, scored 50 in 7 minutes for Gezira against the RAF in 1942. All his runs came in boundaries because he said, 'at my age you don't want to run too much'. Coen was in his 40th year.

Playing for London Counties v Hayes in 1941 the legendary smiter Arthur Wellard hit 50 in 8 minutes. He scored 7 sixes off 9 deliveries.

It took Clive Inman 11 scoring strokes to complete a 50 in 8 minutes when batting for Leicestershire v Nottinghamshire at Trent Bridge on 20 August 1965. The Notts. bowlers sent down full tosses in order to hasten a declaration. Inman's is the fastest 50 in first-class cricket. It was scored off two overs and one ball.

For the Goldsmiths' Institute 'A' Team v New Eltham at New Cross in August, 1901, P Henty scored 10 fours, 2 sixes and a 2 from 13 consecutive balls bowled to him, making a total of 54 in 9½ minutes.

Shropshire paceman, Tom Pitt, scored 64 runs off 20 deliveries with the 50 coming in 12 minutes off 15 balls in a match against Somerset Seconds at Taunton. With Richard Burton he added 73 in 17 minutes.

'Percy' Chapman playing for Hythe Brewery against Eltham Division, Kent County Police in September, 1925 made 183 out of 190 scored from the bat in a total of 201, i.e. 96 per cent.

In a Company game of the 2nd Hampshire Regiment, Capt. A C Richards scored 101 not out and 185, the next highest score from the bat in the first innings being 2 and in the second, 6. Of the 311 runs made from the bat by his side in the two innings, Capt. Richards claimed all but 25. He also took 8 wickets in the first innings of his opponents.

G L Jessop scored 233 at a remarkable rate for an England XI against Yorkshire at Lord's in September, 1901. His first 50 was made in 39 minutes, the 100 was reached in 70, 150 in 100, 200 in 135 and his final 233 (out of 318) arrived in 150. Jessop's last 57 runs (out of 59) took half-an-hour. In a club and ground match for Gloucestershire five months earlier, Jessop had scored a century in 49 minutes with the last 66 runs taking only 19.

In the same year, Jessop had a sparkling partnership with Sammy Woods in a game at Bristol, between Woods' XII and Dr E H Cook's XII. Between them they made 50 runs in 8 minutes, 60 in 10, 100 in 16 and 142 in 22.

'Ted' Boaler Alletson, who was brought up on the Duke of Portland's estate in the Dukeries, created a sensation when playing for Notts against Sussex at Hove in 1911. He scored 189 in 90 minutes, the last 142 coming in 40 minutes off 51 out of 70 balls. Henceforth, considered to be the most outstanding sustained sequence of hitting ever seen in first-class cricket.

Prior to the game Alletson had injured his wrist and that morning in May had gone down to the sea for a bathe in the hope that the salt water might aid its recovery. He had an arm-span of 6 ft 6 in and used it to advantage when hitting Killick for 22 off one over and 34 off

another. At one point there were five balls 'lost' outside the ground and consequently precious seconds (for statisticians) were spent in fetching replacements from the pavilion.

Alletson is quoted as saying, 'After lunch, A O Jones told me to have a go, so I did. Runs kept coming and I cast care aside and hit harder.' Most of the sixes were hit over mid-on, five of them over the South Stand, some carrying to the skating-rink, some as far as the hotel, one ball through the clock-face, another that smashed the pavilion window and wrecked the bar and yet another that had to be prised out of the news-stand into the soft wood of which Alletson had driven it.

Schoolboy Gary ('Chaka') Watson scored 204 in a Johannesburg under-18 competition match on January 2, 1963. His first century took 45 minutes and the remaining runs 48 minutes – all before lunch.

David Whatmore scored the fastest recorded double century in all forms of cricket in Alderney in 1983. Playing for the Channel Island against Sun Alliance he pulverized the attack to the tune of 210 off 61 balls, including 25 sixes and 12 fours. The club rapidly used up the supply of balls as many were hit over the cliff.

By the end of the 1967 season, J P F Misso had scored 284 centuries.

The only batsman to score a double century in both innings of a first-class match is Arthur Fagg. Playing for Kent against Essex at Colchester in 1938 he scored 244 and 202 not out. Fagg's feat has been matched in minor cricket:

W B Souness, 201 and 201, Narrikup v Centrals, Mount Barker, Western Australia, 1983.

S Saleem, 210 and 301, All Saints High School v Madraca-I-Aliya School, Hyderabad, 1962–63.

R A A Beresford, 102 not out and 307 not out, School House v Laxton House, Oundle School, 1888.

In 1935, L W Newman scored 4,138 runs in club cricket which is possibly the world record for a season in this class of the game.

Quiz question: What have J C Sharp, D R Havewalla, C J Eady and A E J Collins got in common? Answer: They have all scored over 500 runs in an innings. Sharp made 506 not out for Melbourne Grammar School against Geelong College at Melbourne during the 1914–15 season; Dady Havewalla, a left-hander with a reputation for big hitting, scored 515, including 32 sixes and 55 fours for the BB and CI Railway against St Xavier's College in a Times of India Shield match at Bombay in December 1933; solicitor Charles Eady, 6 ft 3 in tall and weighing 15 st, hammered 566 out of a total 908 in under eight hours for Break O'Day v Wellington in March 1902; and, of course, the most remarkable individual innings in minor cricket, Arthur Edward Jeune Collins, later to become a Lieutenant in the Royal Engineers and who was killed in the First World War, 628 not out for Clarke's House v North Town in a junior house match at Clifton College spread over four afternoons in June 1899, when he was only 13 years old. The innings took, in all, 6 hrs 50 min and included a 6, four 5s, thirty-one 4s, thirty-three 3s and one hundred and forty-six 2s, and was out of a total 836. For good measure, Collins also took 11 wickets in the match and his side won by a huge margin, an innings and 688 runs.

In 1947/8, K C Ibrahim made 709 between dismissals, a world record.

Yet another who has made over 500 in an innings was C L Malhotra in 1956/7. He scored 502 not out for Mahendra College v Government College, Rupar at Patiala and then in his next 2 innings, he made 360 and 144, a total of 1,006 runs in 3 consecutive innings, unequalled in any class of cricket.

BOWLED OVER

On 8 September, 1883 the *Brighton Herald* published the following: 'After an illness of several months Mr Thompson, who in his younger days gained considerable celebrity as a cricketer, died at East Hoathly on Monday at the advanced age of 91 years. It is recorded of him that on one occasion he executed the extraordinary feat of taking thirteen wickets with thirteen successive balls displacing the middle stump with each.' Who said thirteen was unlucky! Well, nobody is on record as matching that incredible display though some have come close.

Jehangir H. Elchidana took 11 for 21 in an innings for New High School v Elphinstone College 'B', at Bombay in 1904.

T A Higson took 11 for 31, all the wickets in a 12 a side match for A E Lawton's team against that of E M Wilkins in September, 1901.

May 1924: J W Brockley (aged 17) took all 10 wickets, clean bowled, in 11 balls, including a triple hat-trick in an inter-divisional match at

Purfleet in Essex. He gave away two runs.

Jennings Tune was on song in May 1922, when in 5 overs for Cliffe, Yorkshire against Eastrington he took all 10 wickets, again all bowled for no runs.

Thirteen-year-old D Norquay took 10 for 0 in an innings in a Sydney junior cricket match during the 1966–67 season. Around the same time 11-year-old C Bardrick also captured 10 wickets in an innings – for Taabinga v Nanango – bowling nine of them and dismissing his tenth victim caught and bowled.

Two schoolboys have taken 9 wickets in successive balls, Paul Hugo for Smithfield v Aliwal North in Johannesburg, South Africa in February, 1931 and Stephen Fleming in an inter-school match at Blenheim, New Zealand in December, 1967.

In 1882, the Ashcombe Park professional, Walker, took 8 wickets in 8 balls, which progressed ultimately to 9 in 11 for 0 runs.

A player called Bone taking part in an inter-Services game at Bangalore in 1884 captured 7 wickets with consecutive balls. it is likely that some of his deliveries went 'near the knuckle'.

G Freeman obtained 6 wickets in successive balls for the United All-England against 22 of Redcar in 1866.

In 1893 Pipe-Major Sutherland, playing for Sergeants of the Station v Sergeants of the 11th Hussars at Sialkot took 6 wickets in 6 balls.

Was there a hidden significance in the fact that W E Smith hit the middle stump on each occasion when taking 6 wickets in 6 balls for Married v Single of the Cirencester Club at Liddington in the Spring of 1901?

In 1890 D B Tapia took 5 wickets with consecutive balls during a game between Independent CC and Hindus.

M E Pavri hit the wicket 4 times in 4 balls for Parsis v Secunderabad in 1891.

Twelve-year-old K Wellard managed to take three hat-tricks in one day for Barrach Point against Shellharbour in New South Wales South Coast junior cricket.

The most hat-tricks in an eleven-a-side match must surely be when W Clarke took 3 in the first innings and 2 in the second for St Augustine's College, Ashford v Ashford Church Choir in 1912.

Several bowlers have taken all 20 wickets in a match; some instances:
    F S Spofforth took all 10 twice and bowled each of his victims at

Bendigie during the 1881/2 season.

J Bryant, Erskine v Deaf Mutes, Melbourne, October 1887. Bryan's victims were all clean-bowled.

J Martin, Stockbridge v Abbots Ann, 1883.

C Bashford, Reynard's Road Methodists v St Augustine's Church, Coburg, Victoria took 20 for 24 runs, 1903/4.

A bowler named White took 20 for 37 for Hughenden v Woodcroft at Bristol, 1921.

Lou Benaud, father of Richie and John, captured all 20 wickets for 65 runs for Penrith Waratahs v St Mary's, 1922/23. The game was played on successive Saturdays on two different grounds.

Albert Rimmer, Linwood School v Cathedral Grammar School, Canterbury, NZ, December, 1927.

1932 Y S Ramaswami, Marimallapa High School v Wesleyan High School, Bangalore took 20 for 31 including a hat-trick.

1935 W Doig for Great Fremantle in match at Perth, Western Australia, took 20 for 16.

J E Pothecary, when only 16, took all 20 for Seapoint v Landsdowne, Capetown, 1950/1.

The Grand Old Man of London Club cricket, Charles Absolon, played until 1897, by which time he was 80. In that season he took 100 wickets, which brought the total to around 8,500 since he was 50. Between 1871 and 1893, he performed the hat-trick 59 times.

The outstanding wicket haul in first-class cricket is by Jim Laker with 19 for 90 for England v Australia at Old Trafford, Manchester in July 1956.

Quartermaster-Sgt Miller appearing for Deodalee v Egutpootra in 1876 took 18 of his opponents 20 wickets. In the first innings he obtained all 10 for 10 runs.

Playing for the All-England XI which travelled around the country during the middle of the last century, the ace lob bowler Chris Tinley took all 17 wickets in a match against 18 of Hallam. Quite clearly an occasion when underhand methods gained the upper hand.

The great S F Barnes scored a 100 and took 17 wickets in the match for Staffordshire v Durham at South Shields in 1911.

Pat Pocock made wicket-taking history in first-class cricket during a dramatic spell at Eastbourne in August, 1972. With Sussex needing 18 runs for victory over Surrey he took 4 wickets in 4 balls which progressed to 5 wickets in 6 balls, 6 in 9 and finally 7 in 11, thus equalling or breaking three world records. Pocock's feat of 5 wickets in 6 balls had been achieved twice before in first-class cricket: W H Copson for Derbyshire v Warwickshire at Derby in July, 1937 and W A Henderson for North-East Transvaal v Orange Free State in the following South African season.

John Wisden, founder of the Almanack, though slight in physique, was a formidable all-rounder; resolute batsman and penetrative round-arm fast-medium bowler. He twice took all 10 wickets in an innings and during the 1851 season captured 455 wickets in 43 matches.

Azim Khan captured 10 wickets in an innings an incredible nine times between 1914 and 1927.

CAUGHT OUT

Undoubtedly the most remarkable piece of catching that has been recorded (by G B Buckley in his unpublished *More Historical Gleanings*) was when an anonymous slip fielder for Islington Albion pouched all 10 of his opponents in an innings, all at the same end and off the same bowler. A schoolboy named Barker practically emulated this near-miraculous happening when he too caught all 10 in an innings, for London Schools v Southend Schools at Lord's in 1904. There have been other noteworthy instances.

Stephen Lane, a 13-year-old schoolboy, held 7 catches in each innings in the field – the highest number of recorded catches in a match – in a college game at Lower Hutt in Wellington, New Zealand.

'Pete' O'Neill, playing for Twelve of Germantown v Australia in 1913 – the Americans won by 3 wickets – held ten catches during the match fielding at slip.

In first-class cricket there have been two players, other than wicket-keepers, who have taken a record 7 catches in an innings:– M J 'Mickey' Stewart for Surrey in Northamptonshire's second innings at Northampton in 1957 and A S 'Tony' Brown for Gloucestershire in Nottinghamshire's second innings at Trent Bridge in 1966.

Eight players (again, excluding wicket-keepers) have taken 8 catches in a first-class match, the most recent being Peter Walker for Glamorgan against Derbyshire at Swansea in 1970. The feat has been surpassed once, by W R 'Wally' Hammond for Gloucestershire against Surrey at Cheltenham in 1928. Eight of his 10 catches were held off.the bowling of Charlie Parker and when it was Gloucestershire's turn to bat, Hammond made sure that it was *his* match by scoring a century in each innings. In that same year, 1928, Hammond took the record number of catches in a first-class season, 78.

The record for most catches in a Test career by other than a wicket-keeper is held by Greg Chappell of Australia with 122 in 87 matches. Chappell also holds equal first place for the record number of catches in one Test, 7, against England at Perth, 1974/75. The co-holder of the record, Yajurvindra Singh, also captured his haul against England at Bangalore during the 1976/77 series. Singh took 5 of his 7 catches in the first innings, tieing for the record number held in a Test innings coincidentally with the grandfather of Greg Chappell, V Y Richardson.

Another Australian, Jack Gregory, heads the list of most catches,

 excluding wicket-keepers, in a Test Series. Gregory captured 15 against England in 1920/21.

Frank Woolley holds the fielding record for most catches in first-class cricket, 1,018. For wicket-keepers, R W 'Bob' Taylor leads the list, 1,471. Taylor also collected 175 stumpings in his career.

A W T Grout took 8 catches in an innings, keeping wicket for

Queensland against Western Australia at Brisbane in the 1959–60 season. D E East did likewise for Essex v Somerset at Taunton in 1985. They top the list of dismissals by wicket-keepers in an innings in first-class cricket.

One of the most remarkable catches happened at the Oval in 1880 when George Bonnor, the Botham of his day, skied a ball so high that he and his partner had turned for a third run before Fred Grace, W G's brother, caught it as it at last descended, dropping like a meteorite from above.

The most catches, and at the same time, most dismissals by a wicket-keeper in a Test is 10 by Bob Taylor

for England v India at Bombay during the 1979/80 tour. That Test also saw Taylor equal the most catches and most dismissals by a wicket-keeper in a Test innings, 7. The season before, the Pakistani 'keeper Wasim Bari had caught 7 in an innings playing for his country in a Test against New Zealand at Auckland.

J G Binks, Yorkshire and England wicket-keeper, has taken most catches in a season. In 1960, he was credited with 97 in a total of 108 dismissals. A few years later, many record books revised the figure to 96 in 107. In the same season, J T Murray the Middlesex and England wicket-keeper took 95 catches.

The Australian wicket-keeper, Rodney Marsh has made most dismissals in a Test career, 355, including 343 catches. Marsh played in 96 Test Matches. He also took most catches in a Test Series, 28 in five matches v England, 1982/83.

The most catches taken by wicket-keepers in a first-class match is 11. The feat has been achieved on three occasions, firstly by Arnold Long for Surrey v Sussex at Hove in 1964, then by Rodney Marsh for Western Australia against Victoria at Perth in the 1975/76 season and lastly by David Bairstow for Yorkshire v Derbyshire at Scarborough in 1982.

In a match in Ceylon in March 1953, wicket-keeper W B Bennette helped dismiss all ten batsmen in one innings. He caught 4 and stumped 6 in Mahinda College's game against Galle CC on the Esplanade Ground.

Leonard Crawley, ace golfer and accomplished cricketer, came out to bat for Essex against his former county, Worcestershire, at Chelmsford in 1937. The Worcestershire captain, the Hon. C J Lyttelton, knowing of Crawley's penchant for trying to score off the first ball he received, told his opening bowler, Reg Perks, to pitch one slightly short of a length on middle stump. The accurate Perks did exactly as he was told, with the result that even though Crawley went through with the shot he was unable to stop himself lofting the ball to a giddy height. The leather was in the air long enough for A P Singleton, fielding at gully, to put his hands in his pockets and say 'I'm not taking that', and for Lyttelton to look round his immediate field with a fair degree of urgency and, seeing there were no takers, yell to Singleton, 'Sandy, you've got to take it'. He did.

Frederick Luther Fane, who generally was a poor fielder, safely pouched an unusual catch to enable Essex to beat the Australians by 19 runs in 1905. Fielding directly behind the wicket-keeper just inside the boundary at deep long-stop he caught Frank Laver, who had lofted an extremely fast delivery from Claude Buckenham straight over his shoulder to where Fane was standing.

Most people could name their own contenders for the doubtful accolade of the worst fielder ever – not necessarily the same candidates for the most dropped catches – but, so far, there does not appear to be an historical concensus. In the modern first-class game, with its emphasis on athleticism in the field, there is no place for 'passengers' to hide and therefore the poor fielder is almost entirely absent.

As far as dropped catches are concerned they have, in their time, had a decisive and immediate bearing on the outcome of Test matches, brought about early retirements, caused much heartache and sleepless nights and initiated persistent barracking of offenders for years on end from uncharitable spectators.

Perhaps Walter Baptist Money who, quite naturally, was pre-ordained for a career in the Church, told the most honest story about a dropped catch. Money captained the Cambridge University side in the Famous 'Cobden match' against Oxford in 1870 and at one point remonstrated with Jack Dale who had let an easy chance at point go to ground.

'I'm awfully sorry, Walter,' responded Dale, 'I was looking at a lady getting out of a drag.'

THROWING THE BALL

Throwing the cricket ball has seldom been an exact science, or at least, the measurement of the throws has not. Originally, it was useful as a military discipline, as practise for hurling grenades. There are reports that Janis Lusis, the USSR javelin thrower, used to throw cricket balls in training and reached distances of up to 150 yds. Colin Bland, the South African Test cricketer, was said in *The World Sports Magazine* to have 'been known to throw the ball clean across the Melbourne Oval, a distance of 150 yards'. In 1940 *The News of the World* published part of a letter from 'Old Timer' who wrote that 'some years ago he and others saw Charley Ransome, the famous sprinter, throw the ball 151 yds 4 ft on Turnham Green. Presumably, the distance should have read 152 yds 1 ft! Officially the first three are as follows, though, as can be seen, there is barely an arm's length between them and 'King Billy' could well be in pole position:

Robert Percival, Durham Sands Racecourse, 1882. 140 yds 2 ft The above year is almost certainly correct and not 1884 as *Wisden's Almanack* maintained for so many years.
Ross Mackenzie, Toronto, Canada, 1872. 140 yds 9 in
'King Billy', the Aborigine, Clermont, Australia, 1872. 140 yds (given) Two and a half yards were deducted from the measured distance to allow for deviation in a cotton tape. Several measurements, however, gave 142½ yds.
A E Manly, Herne Hill, London, 1901 138 yds 2 ft
Ian Pont, Cape Town, 1981 138 yds
George Brown, Wolverton Common, Sussex, 1819 137 yds Doubt has been expressed as to the validity of this throw.
Frank Henson, George Kent Works Sports Ground, Luton, 1985 135 yds 1½ ft Authenticated in a letter to *The Sunday Times*, 20 August 1978.
D G Foster, 1909? 133 yds
W F Forbes, 1876 132 yds Forbes was an 18-year-old Eton schoolboy.
D G Foster, 1930 131 yds 1 ft 4 in Danish record of 120.1 metres.
A McKellar, Dundee, Scotland, 1882 130 yds 1½ ft
G Davidson, Clontarf, NSW, Australia, 1889 130 yds
There are a number of other throws around the 130 yard mark that are difficult to verify. George Bonnor, 'the Colonial Hercules' who stood 6½ ft and weighed 16 stone, is reported to have thrown in the region of 130/131 yds and also a heave of 120 yds while standing in a barrel.

EXTRA EXTRAS

There is nothing more aggravating for a fielding side than to give away unnecessary runs with byes, wides and no-balls. In the 19th century extras or sundries, depending on which part of the world the cricket was being played, often formed a high percentage of the total. Rough

grounds and less importance attached to fielding ability were contributory factors.

There were 149 extras out of a match total of 479 in the Oxford v Cambridge encounter at Lord's in 1836 including 45 byes in one innings of 127.

The most wides recorded in an innings in an important encounter are 46, Cambridge University v Oxford University at Lord's in 1839.

In 1840, the three matches between Eton, Harrow and Winchester accumulated 1,227 runs and this included 347 extras–well over a quarter of the total.

In the 1842 Cambridge Undergraduates v Marylebone match at Parker's Piece, there were 143 extras in the match.

In the same year at Canterbury there were 159 extras in a game between Gentlemen of England and Gentlemen of Kent.

A *classy* match between Undergraduates of Cambridge educated at Public Schools and Undergraduates of Cambridge not educated at Public Schools contained no less than 183 extras, in a match total of 569.

In 1880, Bolan scored 678 against Subordinates at North Lirta in the Bolan Pass. Perhaps the Subordinates took their name too literally for they gave away 133 extras – 21 byes and 112 wides – in the innings.

Cambridge University conceded 57 byes during an innings of 539 by Yorkshire in 1884.

Demerara gained 74 extras including 54 byes in their innings of 529 against William Shepherd's XI at Georgetown, British Guiana in 1909.

Kent gave away 73 extras including 48 byes in an innings by Northants at Northampton in 1955. Anthony Catt, the Kent wicket-keeper was found to be suffering from sunstroke.

There were at least 103 no-balls in the West Indies v Pakistan Test Match at Bridgetown, Barbados in 1977. None of the 103 no-balls was scored off. There were probably others that were. Extras totalled 173 in the match.

Almost certainly the most byes conceded off a single delivery in a match with defined boundaries was at Wallingford, when Charles Kortright bowled a rearing delivery that rose so steeply above the batsmen and wicket-keeper that it cleared the boundary without bouncing. The byes given away – 6.

J H Human illustrated the fallible nature of his surname by bowling

an over of 30 balls in a match between MCC and New Zealand at Dunedin in 1935/36. His long over – a maiden, moreover – was liberally sprinkled with wides and no-balls.

As a palliative to all this profligacy it is worth remembering that *no* byes at all were conceded by Somerset when Hampshire scored 672 for 7 declared in an innings at Taunton in 1899. Their wicket-keeper could have received divine assistance, for he was the 43-year-old Vicar of Martock, Rev. Prebendary Archdale Palmer Wickham.

BAIL AWAY

William Justice Ford, a great hitter and one of three brothers who played for Middlesex, was fond of relating how a bail was supposed to have been struck into the air, made several revolutions and then landed back in position on the stumps albeit with the long end where the short should have been. He mentioned also that he knew of occasions where bails, in being dislodged and falling, had stuck between the middle and outer stumps and of one occurrence where the bail had been found in the wicket-keeper's pocket. For matches on the Castle Hill in Scarborough, the wind was frequently skittish and iron bails were sometimes put on the stumps as they could not be blown off so easily. Nonetheless, wicket-keepers, concerned for their own safety, were wary of their use. The longest recorded distance a bail has travelled after being struck by a ball from the bowler is 83 yds 1 ft 9 in at Hobart in November, 1925. Seventeen years earlier, during a Bedfordshire and Suffolk encounter, Morcom bowled Mustard and sent a bail 70 yds 1 ft 6 in.

When R D 'Bob' Burrows of Worcestershire bowled William Huddleston of Lancashire at Manchester in 1911 one of the bails travelled 67 yds 6 in. Ten years earlier the same bowler in the same fixture at the same venue had bowled Lancashire and England captain 'Archie' MacLaren and the bail had gone 64 yds 6 in.

C Benham playing for Essex Club and Ground against East Ham at Leyton bowled A Seaton with a ball which sent a bail 44 yds.

England fast bowler Harold Larwood sent a bail 66 yds when dismissing G W Martin in a match between MCC and Tasmania at Launceston during the 1928–29 tour.

Arthur Mold, whose county career with Lancashire ended prematurely when he was no-balled for throwing, bowled George Lohmann of Surrey at the Oval in 1896 and a bail flew a distance of 63 yds 6 in.

A bail was sent flying 48 yds from the stumps when Mr W Foord-Kelcey bowled Mr W H Hadow in 1875 during a game between Gentlemen of England and Oxford University.

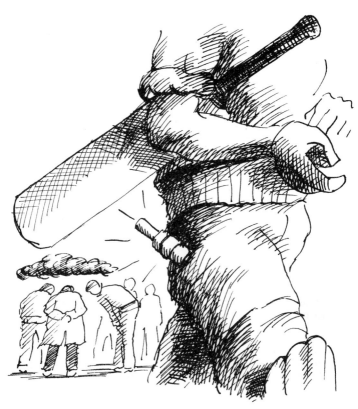

Dr M E Pavri, bowling for the Parsees v Eastbourne and District during the tour of 1888, hit the stumps causing a bail to land 49 yds 8 in away from the wicket.

In a game on the Waverley Oval, Sydney, in December 1900, a ball thrown in hard from the outfield struck off the bails at one end. One of the bails flew the length of the pitch on to the top of the wicket at the other end, dislodging the bails there.

'In furnace-like conditions in a match between New South Wales and Victoria the middle stump was knocked out of the ground but the bails did not fall off. The sun had melted the varnish and they just stuck together.' (Sydney reporter)

A batsman named Winter hit his wicket so hard that 'all three stumps were almost horizontal, but the bails were jammed' and did not fall off. Winter continued batting.

In a match at Cambridge between the University and the Town a ball from a bowler called Reynolds forced a bail 1 in into the stumps but did not dislodge it.

A batsman named French was bowled by a ball which dislodged both bails but the umpire setting out to replace them on the stumps could only find one. After much searching of the ground near the wicket, it was decided to use another bail. When changing at the end of the match, French discovered that the bail had flown into his right-hand trouser pocket.

HOWZAT!

The following include some descriptions of the more unusual dismissals that have been listed in scorebooks over the years:–

Hit ball twice
Obstructed the field
Not out – disabled
Put hand out
'Nipped' himself out
Did not go in, being lame
Retired hot
Gave up his bat (generously wishing to give someone else a turn)
Did not arrive at the crease in time (viz: the two minute rule)
Not out disabled, finger nail knocked off
Left his wicket thinking he was bowled
Retired, thinking he was caught – 0 (J Southerton)
Hurt by Fellows on wrist and refused to go in (refers to the famous William Lillywhite who was then in his late 50s)
Hat knocked on wicket
Dropped his spectacles on wicket
Remembered a previous engagement
Shamefully refused to go in
Ricked his back
Retired, sick on wicket
Incommoded – taken short . . .
Shambled out
Ran away – scared by the bowler
Unfinished owing to disputed decision on the question of lbw
Given out unfairly and refused to retire
Side refuses to go out and abide by the decision of the umpire
Absent batting, 0
G Plank, walked out
. . . not arrived yet . . .
Fison, left to catch a train to the Continent
Sat on wicket
P.M. (pulled muscle)
P.H.O. – 'played himself out', in order to expedite a finish in pre-declaration days
Helmet fell on stumps (Dirk Wellham).

F W Wright was batting for Oxford University versus Gentlemen of the Midlands when he broke his bat as he stroked the ball. Part of the bat leaped into the air, hit him on the head and then fell onto his wicket.

G Streso playing for Uitenhage against Walmer at Port Elizabeth in South Africa hit a straight drive which struck his partner's bat and gave the bowler a dolly caught and bowled dismissal.

G Greenway was dismissed when he drove a ball which hit the head of his batting partner R Clark, thence deflected into the hands of the bowler. The game was one between Holy Trinity and Unley Salvation Army in Adelaide, Australia.

E Dowson, batting at the Oval in 1862, was hit in the mouth by a ball, stunned and knocked on to his wicket. He was adjudged out, 'hit wicket'.

28

In 1898, a batsman in India is reported to have been given out caught through the ball being impaled on the spike of a fieldsman's – a soldier's – helmet.

During the same year in a game at Simla, Captain Onslow received three successive balls which he should have square cut to the boundary; he missed all of them. Onslow was so annoyed with himself that he stamped his foot petulantly and exploded with an unprintable expletive. In the very moment that his foot was off the ground the wicket-keeper whipped off the bails and Onslow was out stumped.

H Charlwood, playing at the Oval, was run out. The mundane entry in the scorebook however disguises extraordinary circumstances surrounding the dismissal. Charlwood hit the ball, gave a catch in the deep which was dropped, ran a second run that was signalled short and was run out attempting a third. Therefore he was missed, made one run, ran one short and was run out all off one hit.

Martin Donnelly, the free-scoring left-hander from New Zealand was playing for Warwickshire against Middlesex at Lord's in 1948. A ball from Jack Young hit Donnelly's foot and then bounced over his head; it landed on a bowler's footmark behind the wicket (that is Donnelly's wicket) and ricocheted back and hit it.

Stories about W G Grace abound and while some are undoubtedly true, some are most definitely apocryphal. Readers can make their own decisions about this strange dismissal that would not be allowed to stand today. Grace was one of the fielding side when the last ball of the day hit the batsman's pads. For some reason, nobody appealed for lbw. During the evening the batsman mentioned to Grace that he thought he had been fortunate to get away with it as he felt sure he had been 'plumb'. The next morning play resumed and before a ball was delivered, Grace squeaked 'How's that?'. The unfortunate batsman, who had spoken too freely thinking he was secure, was adjudged out from the day before's ball.

C I Thornton suffered a strange case of a delayed decision. Playing at Wycombe one Saturday he scored a century. A week later he played there again. He had accrued 70 runs when a ball flicked the flap of his trouser and went through to the wicket-keeper. The umpire acknowledged the appeal with a raised finger. Thornton protested, 'I never even played at it'. 'No,' said the umpire, 'but I gave you "not out" last Saturday when you was out, so this makes it equal.'

George Wells of Sussex was out before the ball had been delivered. He hit his wicket as George Bennett of Kent was about to let go of the ball and the umpire, James Dean, gave the dismissal as Wells was in the act of playing.

A batsman in New Zealand was run out in a peculiar manner. He was running fast to complete a single and in order to avoid being hit by the hard throw-in, he jumped just as he was reaching the crease. His jump took him past the wicket a split second before the ball hit the stumps, but as he was off the ground at the time the umpire gave him out.

A somewhat cantankerous miner playing in an inter-pit game was bowled first ball. He refused to accept that he was out, saying that it was a trial delivery, 'I ain't out,' he argued, 'I ain't out till I'm purred out: happen not then.' An examination of Lancashire linguistics reveals that 'purred' means 'kicked'.

Edward Bowen, much-loved Harrow schoolmaster, who composed the lyrics of a number of songs on the game, once set an examination paper on cricket. He firmly believed that he would have failed in his duty if any of his pupils went out into the world well-versed in 'the doctrine of the enclitic De' but ignorant of the rules of the MCC, or of their possible bearing upon improbable situations.

Two of the questions in the exam were:

a My partner hits high catch. I judiciously tread on bowler's toes, who misses it; then asks umpire to give me out for doing so. Does he?
b If two batsmen walk off simultaneously to have a drink just before 'over' is called, which is out?

Courtney Walsh's magnanimous action in the recent World Cup, in not running out Salim Jaffer who was backing up too far, denied a West Indies' victory, was a salutory reminder that not all bowlers have been so inclined. In a letter to *Wisden Cricket Monthly*, Gerald Brodribb compiled a list of some extremely rare instances when batsmen have been dismissed in this fashion:–

1 G Jones (Surrey) by an Australian bowler, Oval, 1878.
2 C W Wright (Cambridge Univ.) by G P Harrison (Yorks), Cambridge, 1883.
3 E Tyler (Somerset) by A Hearne (Kent), Taunton, 1894.
4 T W Reese (Canterbury) by A Downes (Otago), Christchurch, 1895/6.
5 J Hardstaff (Tennyson's XI) by K Hussain (Sind), Karachi, 1937/8.
6 W A Brown (Australian XI) by V Mankad (India), Sydney, 1947/8.
7 W A Brown (Australia) by V Mankad (India), Sydney, 1947/8.
8 I R Redpath (Australia) by C C Griffith (West Indies), Adelaide, 1968/9.
10 Sikander Bakht (Pakistan) by A G Hurst (Australia), Perth, 1978/9.
11 J Barclay (Sussex) by M D Marshall (Hants), Eastbourne, 1983.

CRICKET DRESS

During the **18th century** three-cornered or jockey hats were popular cricket attire, the mostly gold or silver-laced designs being exchanged for a less flamboyant colour when on the field, i.e. the Hambledon team had dark velvet caps when playing. Historian P F Thomas records that players left their wide-brimmed hats and coats with the scorers, or waiting companions. 'In periwigged London the frock-coat and vest, as well as the peruke, were doffed, and gentlemen played in their ruffled shirt-sleeves with a hand-kerchief tied round their brows, or else "went for it bald-headed".' Frilled and ruffled silk shirts. Sash around the waist (scarlet was a popular colour). Nankeen breeches, nearly always white (the prevailing cricket colour throughout its history). Silk stockings. Silver-buckled shoes (quite dangerous for unwary fielders who could lacerate their hands when stooping low).

Early in the **19th century** trousers began to be in vogue. Black or white beaver hats (Lord Frederick Beauclerk found his useful to stamp

on when he wished to have a tantrum). Shirts less embellished but with high collars, spreading bow ties and wide braces. Singlets were also worn. Belts with ornate metal clasps. Black 'Oxford' shoes.

From **1845 to 1880** soft flannel caps (sometimes straw hats) and short flannel jackets were introduced. Club colours began to make an appearance. Coloured shirts were common and they only gave way gradually to white after blazers (particularly the zebrine variety) became established in the 1860s. White or brown boots replaced shoes.

From **1880 to 1895** starched-fronted white shirts could be seen along with small bow ties and white buckskin boots. The 'sweater' arrived.

From **1895 to c 1975** there was surprisingly little change. Subtle fashion modernizations occurred through the years such as open-necked starchless shirts, rubber-soled boots and sleeveless sweaters. After the First World War skeleton pads were superseded by a less draughty form of leg guard.

From the **mid 1970s to date** some startling innovations took place including the skull cap as worn by Mike Brearley, a plethora of padding without and within, helmets with visors, sweat bands on the wrist (this has been in use by bowlers over a good many years) and the introduction of much specially produced brand-name equipment; prepared plimsolls instead of boots with spikes, coloured shirts and trousers (*a la* pyjamas) for World Series and night games, head bands, etc. etc. The modern cricketer coming in to bat looks as if he is going to war . . .

A CLASS APART

CRICKET AND ROYALTY

'Partly because of the interest in cricket envinced by the Prince of Wales and the games in which he took part, ladies now ride to the Downs to see Earls and great folks play at cricket without having their delicacy wounded, or their finer feelings deranged.' The connection between cricket and royalty if not great, has certainly been eventful.

Sports days were held in many districts annually to commemorate the Restoration of the Monarchy in 1660. Cricket found place in a number of these celebrations and one game at Cranbrook in Kent in 1727 created enormous interest. The idea behind the match was that as many of the participants as possible should have been alive at the time of the Restoration, so onto the field tottered twelve old men – Richard Shere 84, Edward Stone 82, John Honey 82, Anthony Camber 79, Simon Dene 78, John Foul 78, John Buss 77, Richard Harris 77, Nathaniel Rone 74, Thomas Spice 74, William Cropwell 72, James Browne 71. Two more 'ancient oaks' were meant to be there but obviously they had decided to remain rooted to whichever spot they happened to be on, and so the cricketers were obliged to take in Abraham Hitchcock 69 and John Cave 64. Cave was, of course, 'unqualified' as he was under age.

The London Evening Post reported a match played at Kennington, 15 June, 1737:

> Yesterday the great cricket match between His Royal Highness the Prince of Wales for Surrey and

London, and the Lord Sackville, son of his Grace the Duke of Dorset, for Kent, was played on Kennington Common. Kent side went in first and got 99 notches, then the Surrey side went in and got 31; then Kent went in again and got upwards of 70, and three knocked up their wickets; then the Surrey side went in, but wanted 40 of the number got by the Kent side. There was a pavilion erected for His Royal Highness, who was accompanied by several persons of distinction. The press was so great on the occasion that a poor woman, by the crowd bearing upon her, unfortunately had her leg broke, which being related to His Royal Highness, he was pleased to order her ten guineas.

Prince Frederick Louis of Wales, London Club and Surrey, 1707–1751, was fanatically fond of cricket and a generous patron. The heir apparent to the throne apparently died from the effects of a blow from a cricket ball, the injury happening at a game in the park at Cliveden House.

His Royal Highness, the Duke of Cumberland, second son of King George II, once showed himself a poor judge of cricketing ability when raising a side to play the Earl of Sandwich's team. Robert Ord, Chief Baron of the Exchequer in Scotland, explained why in a letter of 1751 to Henry Howard, Earl of Carlisle:

You see in the papers that Lord Sandwich has won his match at cricket against the Duke, but what I think the best part of the story is not told there. The Duke, to procure good players on his side, ordered 22 who were reckoned the best players in the country to be brought to play before him, in order for him to choose 11 out of them. They played accordingly, and he chose 11. The other 11 being affronted at his choice, challenged the elect to play for a crown a head out of their own pockets. The challenge was accepted; they played before the Duke, and the elect were beat all to nothing.

King George III watched a game between Five of Richmond and Five of Brentford on Richmond Green on 17 August 1767, gave a guinea to the winners, half a guinea to the losers and then stood dinner for them all at 'The Feathers' nearby.

George IV, when Prince of Wales, played cricket with Lord Herbert, two sons of the Bishop of Chester and some others, in Kew Gardens in 1772. Apparently, a dispute arose between two of the players, one accused the other of lying, whereupon the Prince ended the game, took the two disputants to the Palace and locked them into a small apartment for an hour, declaring that they were fit company only for one another. The Prince was 10-years-old at the time.

Ex-King George V of Hanover, grandson of George III of England, lost his sight as a result of watching a cricket match. The game was at Windsor, and the then Prince George was carrying in his hand a long beaded purse attached to

which was a gold acorn. He started to applaud a fine stroke and in doing so swung the purse about and the acorn struck him in the eye. Ultimately he became blind.

Prince Christian Victor of Schleswig-Holstein, grandson of Queen Victoria and a member of I Zingari, played most of his cricket in India during the 1890s. He was described as 'a capital batsman and a wicket-keeper of considerable ability'. The Prince once scored 205 for the King's Royal Rifles against the Devonshire Regiment at Rawalpindhi.

The Crown Prince and Princess of Roumania watched a cricket match in Bucharest in 1893. Braila beat Bucharest by 17 runs. Their Royal Highnesses were received more enthusiastically by the crowd than were the players.

Edward VII, when Prince of Wales, played at least twice for the famous I Zingari Club – once against Gentlemen of Norfolk, a game in which R A Fitzgerald, MCC Secretary, scored a century, and once against 22 of the Sandringham Household. In the last match His Royal Highness made 3.

Prince Albert, who in 1936 became King George VI, once performed the hat-trick in the gardens of Windsor Castle, dismissing in turn King George V, Prince Arthur of Connaught and the Prince of Wales.

The grandfather of Princess Anne's husband, Captain Mark Phillips, played occasionally for

Warwickshire from 1904 until 1911. Joseph Herbert Phillips (1881–1951) was a right-handed batsman and fast bowler.

P K 'Plum' Warner's massive tome *Imperial Cricket* was dedicated 'by gracious permission to His Majesty, the King-Emperor'. Published in 1912, copy No. 1 of the de luxe edition naturally was presented to George V. Apparently, he gave the book to the stationmaster at Sandringham. Years later this copy came to light in Brisbane, Australia.

King Hussein of Jordan played

cricket for the Royal Amman CC against a British Embassy team in 1971.

Prince Charles playing for an RAF side against Lord's Taverners at Cranwell in 1971 came to the wicket carrying a polo stick. He scored 10 before losing his wicket to the bowling of Ken Barrington. The Prince then had the satisfaction of dismissing Barrington during a spell of 7 overs in which he took 2 for 37.

The Duke of Edinburgh has been known to bowl 'a crafty off spinner'.

Since the 19th century a number of matches of some note, including games involving I Zingari, have been played at Princess Diana's family home at Althorp in Northamptonshire.

Prince Rainier of Monaco played cricket at Stowe School. 'I didn't like it,' he confessed, 'it was the fielding I couldn't get used to.'

Royal displeasure can take many forms. In a game at Karachi, Prince Aslam, who was renowned for his short fuse, was dismissed lbw. After disputing the decision with the umpire, the Prince was eventually forced to return to the pavilion. A few minutes later, he stalked back onto the field, carrying a loaded revolver which he fired above the umpire's head. Startled players and both umpires fled. The match was abandoned.

CRICKETING ARISTOCRATS

'We are sorry to be so well informed of the conduct of a certain young gentleman near Brighton, and that it is so exceptionable as to have been the means of several of the nobility not visiting that place this season, as they usually have done. Descending to the office of a coachman and driving his own carriage is not altogether compatible with high rank and station, the more so when it is done in a public manner. The making of his own lamplighter a partner at a game of cricket, is equally censurable. It gives us much pain to make these remarks, but as we know this paper meets the eye of the noble character we allude to, we hope the hint will be taken in the same friendly manner it is meant.' (*The Times*, 9 September, 1788)

Horace Walpole neatly damned cricket with faint praise. In a letter to George Montague in 1736, he wrote: 'I can't say I am sorry I was never quite a schoolboy: an expedition against bargemen, or a match at cricket, may be very pretty things to recollect; but, thank my stars, I can remember things that are very near as pretty.'

The Duke of Dorset playing for England against Hampshire at Laleham Burway in 1773 'and having run a considerable number of notches from off-strokes, the Hampshire people very unpolitely swarmed round his bat so close as to impede his making a full stroke; his Grace gently expostulated with them on this unfair mode, and pointed out their danger, which having no effect he, with proper spirit, made full play at a ball and in so doing brought one of the gentlemen to the ground'.

Horatio Mann, wealthy patron of 18th century cricket, once fielded a side whose players included Boorman, Fuggles, May, Love, Bellchambers and Muddle.

The 4th Duke of Manchester caught rheumatic fever from sitting on damp grass when watching a cricket match. 'It baffled all the power of medicine, and after four days' ardent illness caused his death.'

In 1811, Colonel Maceroni, who was much more British than he sounds, 'formed a cricket club in Naples during the French occupation under Joachim Murat, King of Naples, with many French and Neapolitan officers as members'.

In 1815 on 12 June, the Duke of Wellington watched a match played by officers of the Brigade of Guards near Brussels. The Garrison Cricket Club played on the plain of Mons. Membership rules were strict even during war. 'Dress in white jacket and trousers. No member can leave the Game without the unanimous

Lord Byron, in spite of a club foot, played cricket for Harrow against Eton at Lord's in 1805. He had a runner to help him and he managed to score 7 and 2. In the listed batting order he was just below a boy called Shakespeare.

consent of the parties playing and in such case a substitute will be required of the retiring member.'

Charles Lennox, the fourth Duke of Richmond, great-great-grandson of King Charles II and Louise de Kerouaílle, was an extremely able cricketer and a leading practitioner of his day. He played for the White Conduit Club in Islington and later for MCC (he was one of the instigators of the new club) and once scored a century for the Gordon Castle Club v 55th Regiment at Aberdeen in the autumnal gloom of a Scottish October.

The impetuous Lennox fought a duel with the Duke of York and nearly succeeded in blowing his head off. Fortunately, perhaps, for the safety of his own head, he was reconciled with his erstwhile opponent amidst the soothing balm of the sounds of cricket at Lord's in 1790.

Lennox died from rabies in Canada in 1818. His dog, Blucher, got friendly with a fox who did not get friendly with the noble Duke – in fact, it bit his hand and two months later he succumbed after suffering excrutiating pain.

In a match between MCC and Ground and Cambridge University at Fenner's in May, 1865, the Hon. C G Lyttelton had scored 129 when a new ball became due. From the first delivery of the new ball Lyttelton was caught. A month later the same sides played a return at Lord's. Lyttelton had made 35, a new ball was called for and from the first delivery Lyttelton was caught.

During the 1906 season in India, Lord Francis Scott had a batting average that Boycott would have

envied. After three successive hundreds it was 194.00.

Lord Frederick Beauclerk, Vicar of St Albans, great-grandson of King Charles II and Nell Gwyn and one time President of MCC, was not only arrogant but theatrical. He had been known to display his contempt for an opposing bowler by hanging an extremely valuable gold watch from the top of his middle stump.

Sir Julien Cahn, enigmatic and eccentric furniture magnate who died in the 1940s, ran his own team employing a number of county players. He had a cricket ground adjoining his home, Stanford Hall, and the 'Cricketers Wing' of the mansion accommodated visiting teams. Cahn would sometimes practise on the Wurlitzer Organ in the 350-seater theatre below at unearthly hours of the night, which ensured that his opponents would not be seeing the ball too clearly on the following day. He was a man of superstitions who would often turn around three times before passing through a doorway and always put on his right inflatable pad first when preparing to bat. At times when a wicket had fallen unexpectedly, this operation took place virtually simultaneously. An onlooker likened the performance to 'an ostrich doing a courtship dance'.

A SECOND CHILDHOOD

SENIOR CITIZENS

The following trifles owe much to a rare pamphlet by F S Ashley-Cooper entitled *Cricket Veterans*.

On Restoration Day, 1727, twelve men aged 70 or over played in a match at Cranbrook. The oldest was 84.

Six boys, the eldest being 10, beat six senior citizens, the youngest being 70, by 23 runs in a single innings game at Langley, Middlesex in 1778.

It was said of Benjamin Aislabie, who was a central figure in cricket during the first part of the 19th century, that, 'he doats on the game, has played many a year, weighs at least seventeen stones, on his pins rather queer, but he still takes the bat, and there's no better fun than to see him when batting attempting a run'.

Aislabie's last important game was at Lord's in 1841 when aged 67, playing for MCC against Cambridge University. He then weighed around 20 stones and was allowed the services of a runner. The runner was not unduly exerted as the 'big' man scored 2 and 1 not out.

'The Nonpareil', William Lillywhite, was aged 61 when opening the bowling for Sussex against England in 1853. He sent down 11 overs for 23 runs.

As already stated, Charles Absolon took 100 wickets when he was 80 in 1897. Five years earlier he had taken 200 wickets and then, a year later, 209.

W G Grace played his last first-class match in 1908 at the age of 59. He scored 15 and 25 for the Gentlemen of England against Surrey at the Oval.

Wilfred Rhodes was 52 when he played for England against the West Indies at Kingston, Jamaica during the 1929/30 tour – the oldest Test player.

James Southerton was 49 when he played for England v Australia at Melbourne during the 1876/77 tour – the oldest Test debutant.

In 1888, William Adlam aged 104, was one of a team of old-timers in a match at Taunton. He was included to raise the average age and was credited with 3 runs, obtained with the help of a runner. Possibly the world's oldest player.

William Capel was 103 when he faced a few balls on a day's outing to Loughton from a Disabled Veterans Home in Stratford East in 1935.

John Durant claimed to have been a centenarian before bowling for the first time. In 1913, when he was said to be 103, he was afforded the honour of opening the bowling for G W Ayres's side versus Weybridge on Weybridge Common. Off his second delivery a batsman was stumped.

James Oldis was 102 when he played with some youngsters at Eastville, Bristol in 1934. He kept in trim by regularly walking seven miles a day.

Raja Maharaj Singh is reported to have been 72 when he captained for the Bombay Governor's XI v The Commonwealth in Bombay during November of 1950. Maybe the oldest player in a first-class fixture.

C Haydock took an active part on the cricket field for over 60 years. When he was 76, in 1909, he gathered all 10 wickets for 34 when playing for Worksop Thursday against Crossley.

G C Wingham played good club cricket for many a season and trapped unwary batsmen with his cunningly-disguised top-spin. In 1906, he took 265 wickets, in 1907, 266, in 1908, 331 for 8.79 each (also 916 runs) and in 1907, when aged 72, he captured 188 at 10.88. During that year, Wingham's analysis for Folkestone v I Zingari was 16 for 184.

The average age was 75 in a 12-a-side match between Chellour Dene and Shipley at Saltare Park near Bradford in 1914. The oldest player was 87: the umpires were 79 and 75.

In 1927, in Yorkshire, a side of Sheepbridge veterans whose total years amounted to 801, twice defeated an even more venerable team from Bishop Wilton whose ages totalled 836.

E M Grace, brother of W G and known as the 'Coroner', made 351 runs and took 352 wickets for the Thornbury Club in his 66th year.

The oldest umpire in England for many years was Joe Filliston who was born in 1862 and who officiated at club matches well after his 100th birthday.

Filliston who in his youth had played with Grace at Crystal Palace explained his longevity in the following way. 'Well, people often ask me, what's the secret of your "long livity". I don't even know the answer to it – it's just a coincidence. I've always liked me beer and I've always liked me pipe and I've lived in a ordinary manner. I haven't done this and I haven't done the other like people say they are for "long livity". I'm just an ordinary man.'

Filliston finally died at the age of 102 when he was knocked down by a motor scooter.

JUNIOR MEMBERS

The youngest player to appear in English first-class cricket was Charles Young, who was 15 yrs 131 days on his debut for Hampshire against Kent at Gravesend in 1867.

The youngest cricketer to play in a Test Match is Mushtaq Mohammed who was 15 yrs 124 days when he appeared for Pakistan against the West Indies at Lahore in 1959.

WHAT'S IN A NAME

Many players who have taken part in first-class cricket have sported unusual names or, at least, names uncommon to modern sight and sound: **Septimus Coppinger, Theophilus Greatorex, Nelson Zwinglius Graves, Wallis Emerond Evershed** are but a few.

However, **John Elicius Benedict Bernard Placid Quirk Carrington Dwyer,** great-grandson of Michael Dwyer, the Wicklow chieftain, who helped lead the Irish insurrection of 1798, who was a fast bowler for Sussex during the early years of this century, must surely be a front runner in any list of cricketers possessing the most Christian names.

Dwyer astutely maintained friendly relations with the scorers by agreeing early in his career that he would always be referred to as, simply, E B Dwyer.

Fijian scorers must have made a similar pact just after the last World War with **Ilikena Lasarusa Talembulamainavaleniveinakambulamainakulalakembalau.** Fortunately, for the peace of mind of their English counterparts, and also the paper shortage present at the time, Fiji and I L Bula, as he was known, did not tour the UK.

Even the possessor of a name as straightforward as Richard Brooks chose an abbreviated form. The one-time wicket-keeper for Surrey and London County was always known as R B Brooks, even though he had only the one christian name.

NICKNAMES

Players, past and present, tend to get dubbed with a nickname as a sort of calling card, and it is usually a sign of affectionate recognition. Sometimes, though, the name has a short life and is either dropped or replaced with another. A random selection is given below; readers will be able to add many more:

Dennis Amiss
  Sacker
Geoff Arnold
  Horse
C L Badcock
  The Tasmanian Bradman
Robert Bailey
  Dib Dib (Russ Abbot lookalike)
Eldine Baptiste
  Big John
Graeme Beard
  Agatha
Mike Bore
  Noddy
Ian Botham
  Guy the Gorilla
Robin Boyd-Moss
  Mouse
Mike Brearley
  Scagg
Chris Broad
  Norfolk
Ernest Bromley
  Slogger
Alan Butcher
  Budgie
Ian Butcher
  Dog
William Caffyn
  Surrey Pet
Brian Close
  The Old Bald Blighter
Norman Cowans
  Persil
Chris Cowdrey
  Cow
Wayne Daniel
  Diamond

Brian Davison
Shitzu
Kapil Dev
Haryana Hurricane
Graham Dilley
Spotty Dog
Ray East
Spindle
Phil Edmonds
Rommel
Richard Ellison
Bungalow or Plank
Roger Finney
Albert Finney
Keith Fletcher
Gnome
Bruce French
Frog
David Gower
Stoat
Richard Hadlee
Paddles
Rupert Hanley
Spook
Neil Hartley
Hare
Ken Higgs
The Staffordshire Bull
Michael Holding
Whispering Death
Geoff Howarth
Old Bones
Robin Jackman
The Shoreditch Sparrow
John Jackson
The Foghorn
Paul Jarvis
Knasher
G L Jessop
The Croucher
Graham Johnson
Coat-hanger
Ray Jordan
The Slug
Hon. Tim M. Lamb
Tiger
Garth Le Roux
Rocky
John Lever
J.K.
Sir Kenelm Lister-Kaye
The Lion Tamer
Ephraim Lockwood
Mary Anne
Bernie Maher
Action Man

Rodney Marsh
Iron Gloves
Chris Maynard
Fish
Arthur Mitchell
Ticker
Dermot Monteith
Pink Panther
John Morris
Animal Magic
Hallam Moseley
Moses the Lawgiver
Paul Newman
Butch Cassidy
Anthony Nicholson
Teapot
Chris Old
Concorde
Edgar Oldroyd
Little Ack
J F Parker
The Battersea Bradman
Tony Pigott
Lester
Keith Pont
Vintage
Laurie Potter
Bear
Derek Randall
Arkle
John Thomas Rawlin
Turkey-Cock
Dermot Reeve
Huck
Andy Roberts
Fruit
R C Robertson-Glasgow
Crusoe
Arthur Leslie Robinson
Rocker
Joseph Rowbotham
Old Tarpot
Jack Simmons
Flat Jack
John Smith
Soldier Johnny
Graham Stevenson
Moonbeam
Stephen Steyn
Stodgy
Chris Tavaré
Rowdy
G I Thornton
Bun
George Ulyett
Happy Jack or The Big Colt

Derek Underwood
Deadly
Bryan Valentine
Hetty the Hen
Hedley Verity
Clear Gum
The Rev. Archdale Palmer
Wickham
The Bishop
Bob Willis
Goose
John Wisden
The Little Wonder
Arthur Wood
Sawdust or Rhubarb
Barry Wood
Sawdust
Douglas Wright
The Last Cuckoo
Bruce Yardley
The Roo

STRANGERS IN THE CAMP

Virtually every major side in most
parts of the cricketing world has, at
some time or another, contained
players of 'foreign' nationality. Even
in the Test arena there are a number
of quotable instances. In the past, a
bowler of Chinese descent has
played for the West Indies, a
batsman from Malaysia for India,
and recently a Kenyan for New
Zealand. This is not the place to
consider contentious issues like
South Africans of English stock
trying to find an international stage,
or charming curiosities such as
Leslie Compton keeping wicket *for*
the West Indies in a match at Lord's
during the Second World War, or
Guyanan, Lance Gibbs, appearing
for the USA against Canada in 1983.
Nor shall we dwell on the concern
that opportunities for home-grown
talent are restricted because of
'importing' overseas stars. The two-
way traffic between England and
Australia has, of course, been fairly
consistent throughout cricket's
maturity. A non-comprehensive
short list of some post-war English
cricketers who have taken the

chance to capture some warmth
'down under' reads:

G A R Lock	Western Australia
Peter Loader	Western Australia
Colin Milburn	Western Australia
Tom Graveney	Queensland
John Hampshire	Tasmania
Jack Simmons	Tasmania
Roland Butcher	Tasmania
Neil Williams	Tasmania
Gladstone Small	South Australia
Vic Marks	Western Australia
Richard Ellison	Tasmania
Ian Botham	Queensland

Australians have also risked the
vagaries of English weather on the
county circuit; a few that come to
mind are Ken Grieves, Jack Walsh,
George Tribe, Bruce Dooland, 'Jock'
Livingston, 'Garth' McKenzie, Terry
Alderman and Allan Border. Amidst
all this international empathy,
Yorkshire have prided themselves
on their policy of playing only
cricketers born within the county.
Nevertheless, there have been, for
certain, nearly three dozen players
who have managed to evade local
customs. They are:

Thomas Barker – born in
    Nottinghamshire, 15 November,
    1798. Played in 1836.
Thomas Rawson Barker – born in
    Derbyshire, September 4, 1812.
    Played between 1833 and 1849.
William Blackburn – born in
    Lancashire, 24 November, 1888.
    10 Matches in 1919 and 1920.
Matthew Burrows – born in
    Derbyshire, 18 August, 1855. 6
    Matches in 1880.
Brigadier Raleigh Chichester-
    Constable – born R C J Chichester
    in Buckinghamshire, 21
    December, 1890. 1 Match in 1919.
    Captained 2nd XI 1926–1938.
James Cobbett – born in Surrey, 12
    January, 1804. Played in 1835.
Thomas Darnton – born in Co.
    Durham, 12 February, 1836. 15
    Matches between 1858–1868.
Thomas Ellis – born in
    Birmingham, 1 March, 1828.
    Played between 1849 and 1851.

Michael Ellison – born in Nottinghamshire, 1 June, 1817. 4 Matches between 1849 and 1855.

Thomas Foster – born in Lancashire, 12 November, 1871. 14 Matches in 1894 and 1895.

Charles Gifkins – born in Surrey, 19 February, 1856. 2 Matches in 1880.

John Hall – born in Nottinghamshire, 11 November, 1815. 4 Matches between 1844–1863.

Leonard Havers – born in Norfolk, 17 February, 1863. Played in 1890.

Hon. Martin Hawke (Lord Hawke) – born in Lincolnshire, 16 August, 1860. 513 Matches between 1881–1911.

Thomas Hunt – born in Derbyshire, 2 September, 1819. Played between 1845 and 1851.

William Keighley – born in France, 10 January, 1925. 35 Matches between 1947 and 1951.

Charles Landon – born in Kent, 30 May, 1850. 9 Matches between 1878–1882.

Rev. William Law – born in Lancashire, 9 April, 1851. 4 Matches between 1871–1873.

Sir Kenelm Lister-Kaye – born in London, 27 March, 1892. 2 Matches in 1928.

Edward Loxley-Firth – born in Derbyshire, 7 March, 1886. 2 Matches in 1912.

Frank Milligan – born in Hampshire, 19 March, 1870. 81 Matches between 1894–1898.

Cecil Parkin – born in Co. Durham, 18 February, 1886. 1 Match in 1906.

John Parton – born in Shropshire, 31 January, 1863. 1 Match in 1889.

Sir Everard Radcliffe, Bt. – born in Devon, 27 January, 1884. 64 Matches between 1909–1911.

Herbert Rhodes – born in Berkshire, 11 January, 1852. 10 Matches between 1878 and 1883.

William Scaife – born in Dumfrieshire, 3 November, 1830. Played in 1861.

Rev. Charles Sharpe – born in Hertfordshire, 6 September, 1851. 1 Match in 1875.

Rev. Herbert Sims – born in Devon, 15 March, 1853. 5 Matches between 1875–1877.

William Smith – born in Co. Durham, 1 November, 1839. 11 Matches between 1865–1874.

Ronald Stanyforth – born in London, 30 May, 1892. 3 Matches in 1928.

Frank Sugg – born in Derbyshire, 11 January, 1862. 8 Matches in 1883.

Walter Sugg – born in Derbyshire, 21 May, 1860. 1 Match in 1881.

Harry Verelst – born in Cheshire, 2 July, 1846. 3 Matches in 1868 and 1869.

William Whitwell – born in Co. Durham, 12 December, 1867. 10 Matches in 1890.

Anthony Wilkinson – born in Co. Durham, 28 May, 1835. 5 Matches between 1865–1868.

OPPOSING SIDES

'On Saturday, August 10th, 1751, in the Artillery Ground, the first grand match between the Romans and the Hodmandods, in which the Romans were defeated; but being desirous of retrieving their ancient credit (of Veni, Vidi, Vici) have agreed to play the second grand match this day (August 15th) on the second field beyond the White Conduit, Islington. The wickets to be pitched at 1.30 p.m. precisely, by their humble servant, *W.C.*'

At Colchester a brandy merchant played a game against three master hairdressers – the merchant 'ran more notches at one innings than all the gentlemen of the puff did in their two'.

A Grand Alphabet Match was arranged in 1788 between players whose surnames began with letters

from among the first 12 in order, and those from the last 12. At that time the alphabet consisted of 24 letters, I and J being regarded as one, the same applying to U and V.

The City Waiters played the West End Waiters at Lord's on 20 September, 1902, the former being in evening dress and the latter in cook's costume. The *Daily Telegraph* reported that 'The game was in no sense intended to be comic, for the teams played with a keenness which is seldom, if ever, seen on a cricket field. To the spectators, however, the whole proceedings were a huge joke, so much so that the players became irritated at the universal hilarity.'

In 1798, a match was played at Stroud in Kent between two pick-up XIs. One was called the Groutings of the Parr's Head Porter Shop and the other was the Fag End of Rochester Cricket Club. The Fag Ends gave the Groutings 'a severe basting'.

The Whiskey Drinkers beat the Teetotallers in a match at Ballinasloe in 1840. 'After a well contested game, the patrons of the mountain dew won the match by 35, and celebrated their victory in the evening by illuminating their houses, bonfires, etc.'

During the 1886/87 season in Australia, Smokers played Non-Smokers at East Melbourne. This was the match in which W H Scotton was out 'handled the ball'.

'In 1872 in Allahabad, the Pretty Men beat the Ugly Men – twice.'

Brentwood Coachman played Brentwood Gardeners at, not surprisingly, Brentwood.

On one occasion a Surrey side that beat Kent consisted entirely of players named Wood.

Marcus Williams in *The Times* compiled what he considred was the ultimate 'goat' eleven. None of the team batted, bowled or took a catch. The order is alphabetical:

1   I J Coulthurst
    (Lancashire, 1919)
2   T S Fox
    (Middlesex, 1905)
3   J T Griffiths
    (Nottinghamshire, 1891)
4   T J Hearne
    (Middlesex, 1908)
5   F J Hyland
    (Hampshire, 1924)
6   H Longland
    (Northamptonshire, 1907)
7   J L Matthews
    (Gloucestershire, 1872)
8   W E Mirehouse
    (Gloucestershire, 1872)
9   R J Richards
    (Essex, 1970)
10 A J Ricketts
    (Somerset, 1936)
11 W R Thomas
    (Somerset, 1928)

Hearne was appointed captain by the *Times Sporting Diary* because 'not only did he fail to bat or bowl but he didn't field either'.

Lowest Scores and Largest Winning Margin

Ross County (who batted one man short) were all out for 0 on May 30, 1964, when playing against Elgin in a North of Scotland match. B Woolfson took 5 for 0 and D Murray 4 for 0. Elgin had batted first and made 145 for 5.

Wooley CC were dismissed by Earley CC in 34 balls for a total of 1 bye in May, 1901. Previously, East Lothian County had been dismissed for 4 in 1883 and Bute County had totalled 3 in 1895.

City stockbroker Tim Lowdon was out for a walk one Saturday in July 1974. When passing by the cricket ground he found the local side, Whitchurch, were a player short. After agreeing to play he made the top score for the side in their game against Mortimer Farmers. As Whitchurch made a total of 1 in reply to the Farmers 115, it is not difficult to guess Lowdon's score.

The largest winning margin in a 3-day match was established at Lahore in an Ayub Trophy game between Pakistan Western Railways and Dera Ismail Khan, December '64.
   Railways made 910-6 declared (Parvez Akhtar 335, Javed Babar 200, Aijaz Hussain 124, M Sharif Butt 100). They then dismissed their opponents for 32 and 27 (Ahad Khan 9 for 7), winning by an innings and 851 runs.

A match between Eccentrics and Egocentrics lasted 52 hours. A total of over 3,000 runs was scored.

A side called The Untouchables played 127 games of which 109 were lost and the remainder drawn. On one occasion with 6 wickets in hand they needed only 9 runs to win. They failed to score them.

In 1987, *The Guardian* ran a short series on 'Unsung Cricket Teams of Our Time'. Some novel names were forthcoming:

Mk. 3 Cortinas with Fluffy Dice (A Southampton scratch XI)

Chiswick Flyovers (A West London XI with a squad member called M Fore.)

The Lionel Length XI (Based at Parliament Hill.)

Blakes XI (Commemorating TV programme, *Blake's Seven*. Usually fielded 9 or 13 players, thereby illustrating a similarly poor grasp of arithmetic.)

To be Arranged (A Notts. Indoor Cricket League, Div. 10 team, who mostly gathered league points at the expense of sides that failed to turn up.)

The Battersea Bohemians
The Cheddar Gorges
The Chudley Apes
The Cricket Ears XI
The Grim Reapers XI (Motto: Day of woe and doom impending, everything in ashes ending)
The Inner Urban Stress XI found it all got too much for them.
The Lost Graces
The Maida Vailables
Nelson One-Eyes
The Old Reptilians
The Old Ruffians (prefer to be known as *Old Roughians*)
The Paddington Bears
The Pimlico Pimps
The Salmagundians (once based in Covent Garden)
The Shambling Derelicts
The Sussex Ukrainians

FAMILY TEAMS

'The family which pads up together makes runs together.'

The Lyttelton family of Worcestershire, composed entirely of Honourables, took the field in 1867 to defeat an eleven from Bromsgrove Grammar School. The eleven Lytteltons were the Lord-Lieutenant, his brothers W H and Spencer and eight sons, C G, A V, N G, S G, A T, R H, E and A. Obviously by the time the two youngest arrived – Edward and Alfred – the parents were short of ideas for middle names. Half-a-dozen of the team at one time or another played first-class or important match cricket and Alfred, only 10 years old when the match was played, became President of MCC and a Cabinet Minister.

Eleven cricketing Caesars took the field at Farnham in Surrey, which was where 'Silver Billy' Beldham lived and died.

Eleven of the family of Moulding played eleven of the family of Shapely at Chobham early this century.

The Hemsley family beat Isfield by an innings at Blackboys in Sussex in 1901. Another Hemsley played for Isfield.

The Lovell family took on all-comers at the beginning of the century, often at Tulse Hill in South London. Their eleven consisted of father, eight sons and two nephews.

At the Oval in 1910, fifteen members of the Abel family totalled 208 and beat a team called Early Birds by 52 runs. Albert Abel, aged 8, son of the renowned 'Bobby', was the youngest member of his side.

The Partridge family from Gloucestershire fielded an entire XI against Birdlip and Brimpsfield as well as providing a 12th man, scorer and umpire. They even had six reserves ready to act as substitutes.

An XI all called Buckingham beat an XI of the Maltravers family by 17 runs in a 40-over match at Huish Champflower in 1984.

There have been a great number of other family sides that have made their mark, including:

The Bassett's
The Bidgood's
The Boyd's
The Christopherson's
The Cooper's
The Edrich's
The Ellem's
The Ford's
The Foster's
The Grace's
The Groom's
The Hunt's
The Jeffery's
The Leak's
The Lubbock's
The Mackay's
The Mason's
The Newhall's
The Robinson's
The Walker's
The Welsh's

and the Tatas, but not, as far as can be ascertained, the Cobleys et al . . .

AWAY FROM THE GAME

In spite of improved wage packets for cricketers, the game brings riches to but a select few. The majority – those who do not tour or coach abroad and even those who do – have or have had winter occupations, either as a temporary fill-in or with a view to the future. The list below is a random choice of jobs past and present (not all the players are currently on the first-class circuit and a couple of pursuits veer towards voluntary work or hobby) intended to show the scope of activity. There is no guarantee that the employment still continues:

EARNING A CRUST

John Abrahams: Manager of a shop.
Jonathan Agnew: Lorry driver and radio reporter.
Younis Ahmed: Owns and runs a travel agency.
Geoff Arnold: Draughtsman.
Derek Aslett: Window cleaner.
John Birch: Runs a building firm.
Geoffrey Boycott: Once worked for the Electricity Board.
Roland Butcher: Insurance salesman. Also worked for Inter-Action group in deprived areas of London.

David Capel: Surgical shoemaker.
John Childs: Signwriter.
Ken Cranston: Dentist.
Colin Crofts: Air-traffic controller and pilot.
Jim Cumbes: Radio Birmingham D.J.
Peter Denning: Demolition business.
Richard Doughty: Ski technician.
Colin Dredge: Toolmaker.
Ray East: Fuel representative.

Phil Edmonds: Business tycoon.
Keith Fletcher: Oil representative.
Bill Fowler: Opposum hunter.
Joel Garner: Telegraph operator.
Geoff Howarth: Petrol pump attendant.
Geoff Humpage: Police Constable.
Graham Johnson: Investment analyst.
Roger Knight: Schoolmaster.

Allan Lamb: Timber representative.
John Morris: Carpet fitter.
Paul Newman: Cashier in a dairy.
John Rice: Engraver of trophies.
Andy Roberts: Fisherman
Keith Tomlins: Stagehand at
    Richmond Theatre.
Glenn Turner: Worked in a bakery.

OFF-PITCH ACHIEVEMENTS

George Osbaldeston, who scored
centuries for the MCC and Sussex,
took 10 wickets in an innings and
won a match at Lord's with a
broken shoulder, surely qualifies as
the greatest 19th century achiever.
He excelled in so many sports and
became involved in so many
extraordinary and colourful
activities that he was known as the
'Squire of England'. Osbaldeston's
curriculum vitae included:

When at Eton, successfully forged
    letters to go shooting and fishing.
Beat the French and Italian Real
    Tennis Champions by using only
    his gloved hand.
Victorious in several boxing
    matches when conceding up to
    four stone.
Refereed dozens of prize fights.
Won rowing races in his 40s.
Outstanding athlete.
Won a wager for 1,000 guineas to
    ride 200 miles in 10 hours.
    Finished with 1¼ hours to spare
    having mounted 27 horses.
Rode in every Classic.
Fought two duels with pistols.
Dispersed a 4,000 strong rioting mob
    with the help of only five others.
Passion for hunting. Skilled
    marksman who once killed 100
    pheasants with 100 shots.
Married at the age of 65. Too busy
    before.
At the age of 66 went 72 hrs
    without sleep racing and playing
    billiards.
Appointed Lt. Col. of local militia at
    time of Napoleonic Wars.
    Reprimanded for organizing sack
    races instead of drill.

MP for East Retford.
In his 80th year, just before he died,
    when suffering from gout and
    confined to a bathchair, he won a
    bet for a sovereign that he could
    not sit for 24 hrs without moving.

Andrew E Stoddart was a natural
all-rounder. He captained England
at cricket and rugger, was a good
boxer, scratch golfer and played real
tennis, tennis, hockey and billiards
extremely well. In 1886, he played
poker all night, went for an early
morning swim, ate a hearty
breakfast and then journeyed to the
Hampstead CC ground for a match
against Stoics. He walked to the
wicket at 11.30 and batted for 6 hrs
10 mins with his final score an
incredible 485. He then went to the
tennis court, played a strenuous
three-set doubles, had a hot bath
and went to the theatre. After a late
dinner he got to bed at 3 a.m. Truly
a classic mixture of on and off-pitch
achievement.

Charles Burgess Fry, of whom so
much has been written, was
probably the greatest all-rounder of
his or any generation:

Triple blue at Oxford (would have
    also gained a blue for Rugger but
    was injured).
Brilliant scholar. Noted writer,
    published his own magazine and
    wrote his autobiography and
    several other books.
Held world long-jump record, from
    1892 for 21 yrs.
Played soccer for England v Ireland,
    1901.
Full-back for Southampton, FA Cup
    Final, 1902.
Played for London County and
    Hampshire.
Captained Sussex 1904–1908.
Captained England in Triangular
    series. Played 26 Tests.
For over 40 yrs was in charge of the

training ship *Mercury* in the Hamble, 'educating youth with a classical sense of values'.

Deputy to the Indian delegation for three assemblies of the League of Nations at Geneva and composed speech delivered by Ranjitsinghji which helped turn Mussolini out of Corfu.

Could have been King of Albania if he had cared to take advantage of circumstances.

Failed several times to get elected to Parliament as a Liberal.

William Cloete, steady all-rounder for MCC, owned and bred racehorses. His horse, Paradox, came second in the 1885 Derby. Cloete was drowned in the Lusitania in 1915.

C W L Bulpett, Rugby, Middlesex, MCC, adopted the pseudonym 'C W Lloyd' for some matches. Possessed of great self-confidence and a gambling nature, he wagered £200 on being able to walk, run and ride successive distances of a mile in 18 minutes. Another time he bet £1,000 to £4000 on doing the same in 16½ minutes. Bulpett won both bets.

Sir William Everard, who opened for Harrow and played twice for Leicestershire, flew his own 'plane, had his own aerodrome and was a pioneer of private flying. He became a Vice-President of the Royal Aero Club and was MP for Melton for over 20 years.

Romilly Holdsworth, stylish batsman for Oxford University and Warwickshire, and Headmaster of the Doon School, Dehra Dun, was botanist on the Kamet Expedition in northern India, which became the first peak of over 25,000 feet ever to be climbed.

Sydney Morland Crosfield, hard-hitting middle-order batsman, originally a fast bowler and, throughout his career with Lancashire and Cheshire, a fine field, was also a solicitor, a good shot with a gun and won the Monte Carlo Grand Prix two years in succession.

The Rev. George Gillingham was a practising Christian in all senses of the phrase. A member of the cloth for over 50 years he played for Gentlemen of Worcestershire during the early part of this century and then for a few years from 1929 became honorary secretary to the County Club.

One winter the River Severn overflowed and flooded the ground and Gillingham, refusing to believe that this was a manifestation of heavenly wrath, in order to retrieve the account books from the now inaccessible pavilion, chose not to walk upon the water but rather swim in it instead. Whether he accomplished the return journey, smiling radiantly, with the books balanced precariously on his head, is not recorded. For good measure, he wrote Elizabethan romances and occupied a condemned public house to teach boxing and Bible to local hooligans.

'Mustard Millionaire' Sir Jeremiah Colman, whose wonderful collection of cricket pictures and prints housed at his home at Gatton Park, Surrey, were featured in an expensive quarto-sized tome in 1941, often used to relate a story about his father, one of the founders of the firm, J and J Colman. 'The family fortunes,' Colman senior said, 'were made not from the mustard people ate, but from what they left on their plates.'

Colman senior was one of eleven brothers who played as a team in Norfolk and though his son inherited his cricketing ability and captained St John's College, Cambridge, it was as a grower of orchids that he made his mark.

Bob Cowper, Australian Test batsman, took part in the world real tennis tournament at Hayling Island in 1984.

Sandeep Patil, Indian Test batsman, is one of several fellow cricketers making a big impression in the sub-continents' film industry. Patil played the lead in a Hindu film with a significant title, *Once You Were Unknown.*

Ian Pont of Notts. and Essex not only threw a cricket ball 138 yards – close to the world record – but is also a baseball pitcher and a qualified art historian.

Hesketh Vernon Hesketh Prichard had a remarkable life. Born in 1876 he was a fast bowler for Fettes, London County, Hampshire, MCC and the Gentlemen at Lord's. He toured the West Indies with Lord Brackley's side in 1904/5 and

captained the MCC team to Philadelphia in 1907. He was an author, an explorer who hunted with the Eskimos and the Patagonian Indians, a world-class big-game shot and as a soldier in World War I was decorated with the Military Cross for 'taking out' German snipers on his own. Part of the citation read: 'he has directly or indirectly inflicted enormous casualties on the enemy'. Prichard suffered an agonizing illness from a rare blood disease and died in 1922 after 14 operations.

Ian Botham, who has tried most things in an eventful career, walked the 880 miles from John o' Groats to Lands End in 1985 to raise money for the Leukemia Research Fund. He then made plans to emulate Hannibal's feat of crossing the Alps on an elephant.

K C Gandar-Dower made the maxims of Arnold Bennett's 'How to live on 24 hours a day' seem almost obsolete. He played cricket for Harrow and at Cambridge, where he shone in the Freshman's Match, and undoubtedly he would have made even greater impact in cricketing arenas but for his many conflicting interests. An amateur squash champion and a lawn tennis international, he in fact represented his University at six forms of sport: real tennis, lawn tennis, Rugby fives, Eton fives, squash rackets and billiards.

Gandar-Dower must have created some kind of record when he played simultaneously in the Freshman's Match (cricket) and Freshman's Tournament (tennis), 'with the connivance of the tennis but not the cricket authorities; he disappeared to play off a round during the early part of his side's innings, with relays of cyclist friends to keep him informed as to the fall of wickets!'

He played cricket extensively for the Frogs, wrote articles and books, was a War Correspondent in various theatres of operations, travelled world-wide, flew himself in a private 'plane to India, shot big game, and imported a team of cheetahs from Kenya to race for speed records on greyhound tracks.

Gandar-Dower was lost at sea through Japanese action in February, 1944. He was 36.

A BAT, A BRIEF
AND MORE

'A catch was hit very hard to point which Mr Adams (*deputizing for The Lord Chief Justice of England*) secured, but the batsman not wishing to leave the wicket . . . appealed to the umpire who happened to be Mr Justice Manisty. That learned judge at once called the eleven in the field and the umpire at the other end, making twelve in all, together and addressed them thus: "Gentlemen, I have the highest possible opinion of your impartiality, your patriotism, your knowledge of the game, your unflinching resolution never to call a ball which is not a bump ball, or any other opprobrious name, but to do your duty without fear or favour. I ask you, in full reliance on your noble qualities, and with a most confident belief in your infallibility, was this a catch or not?" To this stirring appeal twelve replied as one man, "It was". "Then," said Mr Justice Manisty, "all I've got to say is, it's not out!"'
(*Extract, A Law Club Scratch Match*)

Lawyers not only love to be long-winded, they also love cricket, or so we are led to believe. Some of the most distinguished of their kind learned how to tell right from wrong on the field of play. An Attorney-General and Lord Chief Justice has been a President of MCC and an MCC captain who instituted 'Bodyline' qualified as a solicitor. A list of practising and non-practising lawyers who have played in Test matches would include Alfred Lyttelton, A G Steel, 'Plum' Warner, A B Tancred, C B Van Ryneveld, Jeffrey Stollmeyer and Paul Downton. And they, of course, are a relatively small gathering compared to the many who donned 'whites' before a wig: Roger Kynaston, barrister, was one of the earliest amateur cricketers to play on a regular basis. He was Secretary of the MCC for 14 years to 1858. During his time, he is reputed to have taken part in more matches at Lord's than any other cricketer, amateur or professional. A description of his batting stance reads: 'When in position he stood with his legs as far away from the wicket as possible.'

Sir Edward Bray, who obtained a cricket blue at Cambridge and as a slow right arm bowler played 14 matches for Surrey between 1870 and 1878, became a County Court Judge at Bloomsbury and Brentford. He had his gold watch stolen at a Test Match at the Oval.

Herbert Ross Webbe, Oxford University, Dorset and Middlesex, who played during the 1870s, became a barrister at Lincoln's Inn and then devoted the last years of his life to improving working conditions for boys in the East End of London.

He died suddenly while reciting the Lord's Prayer to a class of boys at St John's School, Titchburn Street, on 9 May 1886. In 1889, Prince Christian Victor (another cricketer) opened an Institute in Bethnal Green as a memorial to Webbe.

Charles Lucas Townsend, Official Receiver at Stockton-on-Tees, was the son, brother, father and grandfather of cricketers, who played for either Gloucestershire or Oxford University. A protege of W G Grace, he stepped straight into first-class cricket after leaving Clifton College. Townsend played 162 matches for Gloucestershire and 2 Tests for England. He took 100 wickets in a season on four occasions with slow off-breaks and in 1899 scored nearly two and a half thousand runs as a left-hander in the middle order. That year he achieved the 'double'.

John Richard Mason, described during his lifetime as 'the greatest living Solicitor Cricketer', played for Kent and England and scored nearly 18,000 runs and took over 800 wickets in his first-class career.

Lord Monckton of Brenchley, QC, Harrow, MCC, played in the famous 'Fowler's Match' at Lord's – Lord Alexander of Tunis was the slow bowler – and later he was Attorney-General during the abdication crisis, Solicitor-General, Minister of Defence (he had been a sound wicket-keeper), Paymaster-General and Minister of Labour.

The Third Baron Aberdare, barrister, who as Clarence Napier Bruce played for Oxford University and Middlesex, scored a century in a Gentlemen and Players match and a memorable 149 in 2 hrs 25 mins against Lancashire at Lord's in 1919. An all-round sportsman, he won many tournaments at rackets and tennis and for 20 years was a member of the International Olympic Executive. In 1957, at the age of 72, he drowned when his car fell over a precipice in Yugoslavia into 3 ft of water in a river bed.

Reginald Addington Ingle, solicitor of Bath, captained Somerset for a number of years in the 1930s. A middle order batsman, he scored a century in each innings against Middlesex in 1928.

Malcolm Robert Jardine, an all-rounder who played for Oxford University, Middlesex and MCC, would probably have spent more time in first-class cricket but for working in India where he became Advocate-General of Bombay. Father of Douglas Jardine.

Louis Goldsmith, KC, who played for East Melbourne CC, was one of the first Australian batsmen to cultivate the pull stroke.

An American lawyer called Quinton demonstrated cricket strokes with a baseball bat at a coaching session for youngsters at Philadelphia in 1897. Quinton admitted to his perplexed pupils that he had only played one game of cricket before.

Learie Constantine practised as a solicitor and barrister in the West Indies. He was a successful plaintiff in an action against Imperial Hotels for operating a colour bar.

CRICKET AND THE LAW

COTTON and CRICKET
or
LOVE and LAW

It's of a love story so curious and strange,
And a great Cotton Broker well known on the Change;

He's so fond of cricket the newspapers tell
He couldn't find time for to court a young girl
It was very wicked for Cotton and Cricket,
To deceive a Scotch maid, who loved him so dear.
They first met at Glasgow, and then about June,
He with the young lass fell in love very soon,
She was turned twenty and fair to the view,
And he was a babby about thirty two.
Then up to his neck he fell deep in love,
He called her sweet names like the angels above,
He told her he hoped that the time would soon come,
When the parson would make their two hearts into one.
His love was so hot that he wrote every day,
And three hundred letters he sent her they say;

He promised to make her his own
darling wife,
On a sweet bed of roses to lay all her
life.
Now from Cricket to Love, is a very
queer jump,
But he was so fond of the bat and
the stump
They say that at cricket the bat he
could wield,
And he liked to be tossing the ball
in the field.
When two months had gone he
began to cool down,
Which caused him to be the whole
talk of the town;
He left the poor girl and the reason
he said,
She won't play at cricket, so her I
can't wed.
But the little Scotch lassie was not
to be done,
She thought she would give the old
lawyers some fun;
Altho' into wedlock perhaps she
would jump
She wouldn't be cast off for a bat &
a stump.
She entered an action in Liverpool
Court,
And for breach of promise good
damages sought,
For the judge and the lawyers it was
pretty play,
They were laughing and chaffing
the whole of the day.
Two thousand pound damages now
he must pay,
He'll very soon learn the Scotch
fiddle to play
He's scratching his head and he's
grumbling the while,
Jolly bad luck to the Duke of Argyle.
Now all you young swells do not
play the dunce
If you mean to get married, why do
so at once.
Don't be like the merchant, get
pushed to the wall,
And for two thousand pounds get
nothing at all.   Anon.

The Canadian tourists of 1880 on
their visit to this country were
captained by Trooper Dale who
came under the alias of Jordan.
Shortly before the match against
MCC he was arrested and charged
with being a deserter from the Royal
Horse Guards some years before.
Dale admitted the offence and
revealed that he had emigrated to
Canada, changed his name, married
twice and was now the father of six
children.

He was sentenced to 35 days
imprisonment but somehow
managed to escape from the court
before being recaptured outside.
Dale's efforts at eluding justice were
of no avail as he received a further
300 days inside.

W R Gilbert, cousin of the Graces,
who played for Middlesex and
Gloucestershire, emigrated in
dis*grace* to Canada in 1886 after he
had been caught filching from coat
pockets in a dressing-room.

Samuel Richardson captained
Derbyshire from 1871 to 1875 – an
amateur, naturally – middle order
batsman and wicket-keeper. He
then became assistant secretary to
Derbyshire until 1890 when he
absconded to Spain with £1,000 of
the Club's money. There he lived
under an assumed name until his
death in Madrid in 1938 at the age
of 93.

In November 1952, Miles W Giffard,
26-year-old son of the Clerk to the
St Austell Magistrates, murdered his
mother and father. In 1948, Giffard
had played for Cornwall in the
Minor Counties competition,
scoring 89 runs from eight innings
with a top score of 27 at an average
of 12.71. At the age of 14 Giffard
had been removed from Rugby
School because his teachers had
found him 'extremely odd, without

emotion and impossible to instruct'. A psychiatrist had diagnosed his state as a type of schizophrenia, probably caused by a sadistic 'nannie' who had often locked the infant Miles in a dark cupboard.

Giffard, who had been prevented by his father from returning to London to pursue an infatuation, killed both his parents by rendering a series of blows on their heads with an iron pipe, before tipping the bodies out of a wheelbarrow over the edge of a cliff.

He was apprehended in London a day later, charged, tried, found guilty and eventually executed.

Miss Bessie Stone sued the Cheetham Cricket Club when she was struck on the head by a ball hit out of the ground in 1947. At the initial hearing at Manchester Assizes, Mr Justice Oliver found in favour of the Club, who were not held responsible (Miss Stone had been gossiping at her garden gate when it happened), but at the Court of Appeal the original decision was reversed.

Ultimately, the case went to the House of Lords who reversed the reversed verdict and decided that costs amounting to £2,000 should be awarded against Miss Stone. However, a fund was inaugurated by the National Cricket Club Association to pay off the sum and since then every sensible club secretary insures against damage to person and/or property.

Leslie G Hylton, the Jamaican fast bowler who played in six Tests for the West Indies and toured England in 1939, was hanged for the murder of his wife on 17 May 1955, at Kingston, Jamaica. David Frith, in his informative book *The Fast Men*, writes that it was a calculated ritual killing in revenge for Hylton's wife's infidelity. He shot her through each breast and in the lower abdomen. Hylton did not wish to entertain pleas for clemency – he preferred to die.

Walter Bultell, a 15-year-old pupil at Plymouth High School for Boys, together with several of his housemates, was instructed to roll the ground one morning some 90 years ago. Bultell tripped into a dip or ditch that had been camouflaged with grass cuttings and the heavy roller passed straight over him. He was severely concussed and received a fracture at the base of the skull. An action was brought by the boy and his father, Henry James Bultell, against the School and the case was heard in the King's Bench Division. The Bultells were awarded £380 damages, being £80 for the father and £300 for the son.

By a tragic coincidence, three-and-a-half months after that accident, another of a similar nature occurred during a league match between East Lancashire and Haslingden at Blackburn. A roller was being taken on to the pitch in the interval when again a 15-year-old boy called Walter – Walter Barnes in this case – fell in front of it and the roller passed over his head. He was taken to the Infirmary in what was called 'a hopeless condition'.

'Judge Albert Marck went a little far when he ruled in a provincial Court case in Hamilton that lying down

on a cricket pitch did not constitute loitering.

We assume it is permitted when someone bowls a maiden over.'

(Toronto Globe and Mail, 1980)

A juryman called Houghton from Hammersmith was excused from attendance at the Old Bailey because he was taking part in a cricket week. Houghton supported his plea by saying that he was getting on in years and as this was his last season he was anxious to play as much as he could. His Lordship: 'I think that is a reasonable excuse. Let him be summoned for the next session.'

F C De Saram, a highly competitive strokemaker for Oxford University, Hertfordshire and Ceylon, for whom he was captain in the first half of the 1950s, became an equally able administrator and selector.

He went into politics, was assertive in his views and, in 1962, was put into jail after having been found guilty of conspiring against the Government of the time.

In 1964, Ossie Wheatley, captain of Glamorgan, successfully sued the *Daily Express* and *Daily Sketch* for libel after they implied that by turning up to toss at Colchester wearing a dinner jacket, Wheatley had attended an all-night party and was in no fit state to play cricket.

Pakistan opening batsman, Aftab Gul, played first-class during the late 1960s while on bail for alleged political activities. Gul, a fervent supporter of the People's Party and a vociferous opponent of the military regime, was visiting England when police searched his house in Lahore

and claimed they had found missiles. Gul, fearing for his life, applied for political asylum in the UK.

When an Oxbridge side arrived in Singapore in 1972, two of their players, Simon Corlett and Bryan Hamblin, not only had their passports confiscated by immigration officials but were ordered to get their hair cut!

It was a case of till cricket us do part for Mildred and Michael Rowley of Wolverhampton in 1981. Mrs Rowley was granted a decree nisi on the grounds of her husband's unreasonable behaviour. She complained that he was 'cricket mad – it was not just a hobby – it was a total obsession'. Mr Rowley was

unable to attend the divorce hearing because he was – playing cricket. Asked for a comment, he replied: 'I cannot stop . . . we have to get on with the game.'

Judge 'Bill' Sime, captain of Notts, England Rugby trialist and President of the Forty Club was a prime exponent of flexible rostering. *The Times* obituary in 1983 revealed all:

'In the summer months, by general agreement, when Notts were playing at home, the Divorce Court sat early so that Sime could get away before 11 a.m. to captain the local team; and he holds a record that is unlikely to be equalled of seven successful undefended divorces in which he appeared as Counsel and 42 runs not out before lunch!'

South Australian batsman Tony Handrickan was fined by Adelaide magistrates after resisting arrest following a fracas in the crowd during the third Test, 1982/3.

Dr Israr Ahmed, a Pakistani theologian, would have disapproved mightily of Hesketh K. Naylor (see p. 80). In 1982, he was one of the instigators in a move by the military government to forbid men from watching women's sporting events; unseemly passions might thus be aroused. Sometime later, he aired the view that cricket was 'a game of eunuchs which wastes the nation's precious time'. A lawyer from the Punjab then took up the cudgels and sued Dr Israr for gross defamation of cricket and its devotees.

Clive Lloyd was awarded over £60,000 when he sued an Australian paper *The Age* for an article which implied that the West Indians captained by Lloyd had not tried to win a game against Australia in order that the home side reached the WSC finals. The Appeal Court overturned the decision.

Graham Gooch received £25,000 damages from *The Sun* newspaper after they printed an article by Ian Todd which purported to reflect the player's feelings regarding the 1982/3 tour of Australia. The story, with the headline: 'I couldn't care less about England', was pure conjecture.

CRICKET IN DISPUTE

Disputes during cricket matches can have deadly consequences. An assistant surgeon in the 11th Regiment of Foot, one Lewis O'Hara, had an altercation with a certain Ensign Mahon during a game at Maldon in Essex. The argument over some trivial point regarding cricketing conduct became so heated that they decided to settle the issue in time-honoured fashion with pistols at dawn. O'Hara's shot missed but he was in no fit state to practise his medical skills on himself as Mahon scored a direct hit to the forehead.

William Oscroft, the Notts opening batsman, refused to accept a controversial run-out decision against himself. After an acrimonious exchange with the umpire, Oscroft and his batting partner 'high-tailed it' towards the pavilion and, after it became obvious that no other Notts players were prepared to continue, they were followed by the Yorkshire side and both officials. A confrontation in relative privacy then followed. One umpire called Luck pushed his own by saying, 'Mr Oscroft was unfortunate in not gaining his ground' and the other umpire called Coward was brave enough to maintain that 'the decision stands'. Only the threat of a crowd riot got the game going again.

S A P Kitcat, an accomplished batsman for Gloucestershire, was involved in a controversial decision in 1886 which led ultimately to a law being amended. At that time Law 14 read: 'The bowler may not change ends more than twice in the same innings, nor bowl more than two overs in succession.' Kitcat was captaining Marlborough against Rugby and the umpires were responsible for the irregularity which occurred. Bengough, the Rugby captain, bowled twice from each end and in his second turn from the pavilion end Kitcat was caught at cover for 27. After some discussion, the umpires gave Kitcat out and eventually the MCC, through its secretary Henry Perkins, agreed with their verdict, and principally because of this incident three years later the law was altered to allow a bowler 'to change ends as often as he pleases provided that he does not bowl two consecutive overs in one innings'.

In a match at Sydney in November of 1900 between New South Wales and the Next XV, the aboriginal fast bowler J J Marsh was no-balled for throwing by Curran, the square-leg umpire. Marsh, who had been 'called' in previous games by other umpires, appeared on the second day of the match with his arm in splints and bowled as quickly as ever. Curran then tried to insist that Marsh's wrists also be placed in splints. After an argument and a refusal by Marsh to accede to this demand, Curran left the field in a huff and another umpire took his place.

At the end of a match between High Bridge Hotel and Mount Erica Hotel at Albert Park, Melbourne on 3 December 1961, W J Young, captain of the High Bridge team, struck the umpire E J Mangan. 'He had been crook on some of his decisions,' claimed Young. The blow caused Mangan to spend over a month in hospital and resulted in Young being sentenced to two months' imprisonment.

The appointment of Javed Saeed of Punjab University to captain the Combined Universities in the 1962–63 Quaid-i-Azam Trophy matches caused friction. Some of the players from Government College, Lahore, showed their resentment by declining to play on the morning that the match against Karachi Blues was due to begin – in effect, going on strike. Not surprisingly the handicap proved too much and Karachi Blues won by 9 wickets.

In a game between Peak View and Railway at Cooma in the New South Wales country League during the 1966–67 Australian season, the umpire ordered a square-leg fieldsman off the field for calling out and encouraging a batsman to take a risky run. The Monaro Cricket Association later issued a statement in which they said that 'the umpire had acted outside the laws of cricket but that no disciplinary action was warranted against any person involved'.

A real cricketing conundrum arose when a match between two sides in Jamaica was abandoned in acrimony.

The ground was adjacent to a busy road and when one of the batsmen hooked the ball he was nimbly caught by an intrepid traffic-dodging fieldsman in the middle of the thoroughfare. The first reaction of the umpire was to award a six; his second reaction was to give the batsman out. Result: considerable confusion, much protestation, lots of unfriendly feeling and quick termination.

Ultimately, the grandiosely named Ocho Rios Hotel Cricketers Association committee were asked to adjudicate. They decided the public road was part of the playing area and therefore the batsman was out.

The local *Daily Gleaner* concluded if a jay-walking fielder happened to be run over whilst trying to catch a ball, the driver would be arrested not only for manslaughter but for trespass as well.

The aggrieved captain of the side who lost the verdict suggested that traffic lights should be installed on the road with 'an impartial cop to switch on "red" when a six is coming'.

Two villages in the Fiji Islands decided to settle their differences by means of a communal duel at cricket. Practically every man and boy in both villages was rounded-up, to make 50-a-side. The fieldsmen covered every area where runs were conceivable – a few even standing and sitting on the branches of trees and others on roofs of thatched huts – so that scoring was nigh impossible. The batting side managed one run between the 50 of them and then, when it was the turn of the opposition to wield the willow, they did no better. A tie – one run each. A compromise? Or differences continued?

CRICKET'S CASUALTIES

It may come as a surprise to some that such an ordered and 'gentlemanly' game can attract so many injuries and, indeed, not a few fatalities.

ON THE FIELD

On 28 August, 1624, Jasper Vinall, a husbandman from West Hoathly, Sussex, received a 'mortal wound on the front of his head and he died on 10 September'. Jasper was playing cricket with various other men on the green at Horsted Keynes when he tried to catch a lofted hit from Edward Tye. Tye, another husbandman from the same village, aimed to strike the ball again with his bat as it was falling to the ground (a legitimate action in those days) and in attempting to do so unwittingly clouted the unfortunate Vinall full in the face as he came running in from behind his back.

At a game in Sussex in 1737, two batsmen collided in mid-pitch whilst taking a risky single. They both fell down and got up but one dropped dead as he struggled to regain his ground.

In a match at Portsmouth in 1796, a batsman called Coulson was hit by a ball and had his eye entirely struck out of the socket.

Alfred Mynn, the greatest all-rounder of his day in the 1830s and 40s, was once injured by a ball from a fast bowler called Redgate. Mynn batted on bravely and made a century but then was experiencing such pain as to necessitate him being led away and lain full length on the roof of a stage-coach rather than sit inside.

A most unlikely fatality occurred in a single-wicket match at Nowgang, India in 1866 between two soldiers of the 7th Royal Fusiliers. The batsman hit the ball and ran. His opponent fielded it and ran with the ball to the wicket, knocked a stump out of the ground causing it to turn upside down and, at the same time, slipped and fell. The brass point of the stump perforated his neck and he died within ten minutes.

Lord's was the scene of what transpired to be a fatal accident in June 1870 when George Summers was hit by a ball from John Platts in the match between Notts and MCC. Summers died four days later.

During the 1870s at a match in India, a wicket-keeper called Arthur Scott was struck by the ball which split his tongue all the way down. He died soon afterwards.

A tussock of grass once caused the death of a cricketer who, fielding in the outfield, tripped over it, ruptured himself and died as a consequence.

A C M Croome, the Gloucestershire cricketer and a notable athlete, suffered a hideous accident when fielding at Old Trafford in 1887. In attempting to stop a ball travelling over the boundary at the Stretford End, he impaled himself in the spiked railings severely gashing his throat. Croome's life was without doubt saved by Dr W G Grace, who held the jagged edges of the wound together in a vice-like grip with his hands perfectly still for over half-an-hour until help arrived.

Misfortune struck many times in a match at Melbourne in 1897 between NSW and Victoria. McLeod, who had been picked to play stood down because of an injured finger and Trott, called in at the last moment, was debilitated by acute indigestion. Gregory hurt his hand and retired from the fray and then on his return the following day was overcome by sunstroke. The rays were too much as well for Noble and Kelly and the latter was too unwell to bat in either innings. Trott, when batting, felt faint and had to leave the field and McMichael collapsed at the end of the game and remained unconscious for several hours.

Eleven of the thirteen players on the field and the two umpires were thrown to the ground when lightning struck at a match between Mirboo South and Glendale in Australia. P C T Meehan who was watching the game was also struck and seriously injured.

In 1902, in a match at Bangalore, a player fielding at deep cover-point was knocked over and stunned by the blast from a gun which was always fired at noon.

'It was reported that, in a match at Rajkot in 1906, Captain Pogson, after bowling the fifth ball of an over, sat down on the crease and died before he could be taken into the pavilion.'

An umpire called John Maycock died as a result of one of his decisions. During a match at Barton-Segrave an altercation followed one of his rulings, whereupon he had a fit and was taken home. Another seizure followed and subsequently Maycock was found dead in bed.

F Henry, captain of Holborn Cricket Club, died from a blow by a cricket ball on a varicose vein.

In 1906, during a match at Blickling in Norfolk, a batsman straight-drove the ball back to the bowler hitting him on the shin and breaking his leg.

In the same year, 11-year-old Herbert Cuttingham was hit behind the ear by a cricket ball while playing on Wandsworth Common. He died the next day due to compression of the brain following a fracture of the skull.

Again in 1906, Samuel Patient, a butcher by trade, was struck under the left ear while batting for Little Waltham v Chelmsford Grammar School. The ball bowled by a master of the school killed the unfortunate Patient.

A certain T Cartlick, while batting for Woore in Shropshire, suffered a heart attack and died on the spot. At his funeral the floral tribute sent by the club was in the Woore colours, yellow and green, and made into the shape of two wickets, two bats and a ball. It bore the inscription: 'Not Out'.

At a match at Leyton one day play became rather tedious causing a gentleman in the pavilion to yawn so hard that he put his jaw out. A doctor, taking part in the game, was summoned to restore the jaw to its usual position in order that the bored watcher could eat his lunch.

Andrew Ducat, Surrey and England and also a soccer international died in action. On July 23rd 1942, aged 56, he experienced a heart attack while batting for Surrey Home Guard against Sussex Home Guard at Lord's.

Abdul Aziz, a 17-year-old Karachi wicket-keeper and an employee of the State Bank, was batting during the final of the Quaid-i-Azam Trophy in January, 1959. *Wisden* records that 'after being struck over the heart by a slow off-break from Dildwar Awan, the Combined Services bowler, he was preparing to receive the next ball when he fell to the ground. He died on the way to hospital without recovering consciousness.' The brevity of the scorebook entry matches poor Abdul's brief, untimely claim to fame:

First Innings: Abdul Aziz retired hurt, 0
Second Innings: Abdul Aziz did not bat, dead 0

Lightning struck to the ground fifteen participants in a game at the Harlequin Club, Pretoria, South Africa in 1959. On the fielding Pelican side, both batsmen and umpires were dazed but not seriously hurt.

N J Contractor, the Indian opening left-hand bat and captain, had his Test career prematurely terminated when a ball from Charlie Griffith fractured his skull in a match between India and Barbados during the 1961/62 tour of the West Indies.

Ewen Chatfield, the New Zealand number eleven batsman, deflected a bouncer from England's Peter Lever on to his left temple during the first Test Match at Auckland in February, 1975. Chatfield, on his Test debut, had scored 13 at the time and was knocked unconscious. Bernard Thomas, the physiotherapist with the England team, rushed onto the pitch and gave Chatfield heart massage and mouth-to-mouth resuscitation. Later the injured batsman was taken to hospital. Thomas said that Chatfield's heart had stopped beating for several seconds. 'It was the worst case I have seen and I never want to see another.'

A Police Constable died after being kicked while trying to stop a brawl during a match between Tasmania and Queensland at Hobart in 1982.

The Graphic of 20 February, 1886, reported an alarming story from Salisbury Plain on the island of St Helena. During a recent match, a fielder had chased after a long hit with such alacrity that he had been unable to stop himself toppling over the edge of a cliff. He fell to his death on the rocks below.

During the final Test of India's visit to the West Indies in 1975/76, there were so many injuries caused by the four-man Caribbean pace attack that the tourists used all 17 of their players. One substitute, Surinder Armanath, was not a victim of the bowlers; he went down (perhaps to his relief) with appendicitis.

A 20-year-old umpire called Mr Pimple gave a disputed decision in a match at Nagpur in India two days after Christmas, 1987. The wicket-keeper took umbrage and hit Mr Pimple over the head with a stump. The unfortunate Mr Pimple suffered more than a burst namesake. He died shortly afterwards from severe head injuries. The wicket-keeper vanished.

Albert Trott bowled far too well at his own benefit match. Having destroyed Somerset with his medium pace off-breaks the game finished early, thereby losing a great deal of potential gate-money. Lamented Trott: 'I've bowled myself into the workhouse.' Prophetically his words came near the truth. He was soon to be onset by poor health and financial worries which in the end led to suicide.

The most 'gentlemanly' of games has sparked what has been described as 'the ultimate crime'. After a dissension-strewn game in Karachi in 1987, two brothers, Alimuddin and Nazimuddin attacked members of the opposing team. Two were killed having been shot and two were injured by stab wounds.

OFF THE FIELD

A ticket porter, crossing Upper Moorfields one Monday in 1766, had his eye knocked out by a cricket ball.

One year later, a horse pulling a chaise past Kew Green was struck on the side of its head by a violently driven ball causing it to collapse on to the ground and overturn the chaise with its occupants.

In September 1858 one of the best single-wicket players in the country, Thomas Hunt, lost his life in a gory fashion. Shortly after the end of a match in which he had been playing, between 11 of England and 20 of Rochdale, he decided to walk up the adjoining railway line to the local station and was run over by an engine, which sheared off both his legs and the fingers of his left hand.

At Princes' Ground in 1876, the old Sussex wicket-keeper, Tom Box, was sitting near the scorebox watching Middlesex play Nottinghamshire. Suddenly he suffered a heart attack and fell dead. The match was ended abruptly.

George Spillman, wicket-keeper, who played for Middlesex in 1886 and then later became a coach in Jersey, had his cricket career terminated in a most unfortunate way. He slipped down the cabin stairs of a passenger steamer and his right leg was damaged so badly that it had to be amputated.

Billy Bates, popular Yorkshire all-rounder, had his career in cricket finished in a most unfortunate and painful way. During the tour of Australia in 1887/8 with Vernon's side, he was bowling in the nets at Melbourne to wicket-keeper Blackham. In an adjoining net 'Billy' Newham was facing George Brown, both members of the other touring team to the Antipodes under the aegis of Shrewsbury, Shaw and Lillywhite. Just as Bates began his run-up, Newham hit a tremendous drive which sailed out of the net and caught the unlucky Yorkshireman with terrible force just under the right eye. His sight was permanently damaged and on his return to England, despondent at sudden obscurity after years of public acclaim, he tried to take his own life. Happily, he was unsuccessful and later managed to do some coaching.

Ex-Harrovian John Dunn, who played for both the Gentlemen of England and the Gentlemen of Ireland and toured North America with the latter, eventually took up residence in Hong Kong. A hefty hitter of the ball, he joined Hong Kong CC, became known as 'the Grace of the East', and played in the annual match with Shanghai in 1892. On the return voyage he and the rest of the team were drowned when the SS Bokhara was shipwrecked off Sand Island, Formosa, during a storm.

William Brereton Evans, all-rounder for Oxford University, Worcestershire, Hampshire and the Egyptian Civil Service, died in a flying accident with aviator Colonel Cody at Aldershot in 1913 at the age of 30.

Thomas Campbell, reserve wicket-keeper for South Africa on their tour of England for the Triangular Series in 1912, appeared to be jinxed by trains. In 1916 he fell out of the Cape mail train from Johannesburg and was picked up unconscious by the driver of a subsequent goods train. Campbell sustained such serious head injuries, apart from concussion, that for a long time the staff at Krugersdorp Hospital thought he would not recover. Eight years later he met his death at Milndale in Natal when the morning up-mail train from Durban was involved in a railway accident.

Gilbert Jessop underwent a frightening experience in May 1916. Suffering from lumbago and wanting to lose weight, he visited a clinic in Bath and was put into a 'sweat box', one of those contraptions where only the head remains visible. The lid of the container can normally be easily lifted from inside, but in this case the catch had fallen into a locked position and poor Jessop was quite unable to get out. The attendant had gone away, or at any rate was not in earshot, and the desperate 'patient' was left to 'broil' for a dangerously long time before being released from his ordeal. The experience permanently weakened his heart.

J W H T Douglas, Olympic middleweight boxing gold medallist, amateur soccer international and captain of Essex and England at cricket, was drowned while attempting to save his father when the Finnish ship on which they were aboard, *Oberon*, sank after a collision with its sister ship, *Arcturus*, in dense fog, in the Kattegat in December, 1930.

William Whysall, opening bat, medium pace bowler and wicket-

keeper, who played for Notts for 20 years from 1910 and also in four Tests for England, died from blood poisoning after a fall on a dance floor when only 43 years old.

The same fate befell Donald Eligon, one of the outstanding bowlers in the West Indies, though in his case the poisoning was caused by a rusty nail in his cricket boot. He was 28 at the time of his death in 1937.

The attractive cricket green at Chipperfield in Hertfordshire has a track alongside one boundary on which spectators park their vehicles to watch the game in progress. In May, 1986, an ice-cream van was also parked on the track and a gentleman of advanced age, with his back to the cricket, was just purchasing a '99 ice-cream when a mighty six struck him right between the shoulder-blades, causing him to come face to cone with his ice-cream. As he turned round bruised and angry, the concern of people nearby turned to mirth. The stricken gent's visage was that of a circus clown, emphasized by the chocolate flake, which was stuck at a crazy angle up his right nostril.

Acting Squadron-Leader Claude T. Ashton, one of the well-known cricketing *brother*-hood, who played for Cambridge University and Essex, was killed on active service with the RAF in Wales in 1942 when the 'plane he was flying collided with another that was being piloted by Squadron-Leader R de W K Winlaw, Cambridge University and Surrey.

Hedley Verity of Yorkshire and England, Captain in The Green Howards, died of wounds received during the 8th Army's first attack on the German positions at Catania, in Sicily in 1943.

Stanley McCabe, the great Australian batsman, died when he fell from a cliff at Beauty Point in 1968.

'Reg' Bettington who, in 1923, became the first Australian to captain an Oxford University side, leg-break and googly bowler for Middlesex and New South Wales, winner of the Australian Golf Championship, ear, nose and throat specialist to Hawke's Bay Hospital, had a fatal accident when his car fell 100 ft on to a railway line in New Zealand in 1969.

A Hackney inquest returned a verdict of accidental death on 12-year-old Edward Henry Ruff who was killed when falling from a 30 ft high rainpipe at the side of a house as he was trying to recover a cricket ball that had lodged on the roof.

CASUALTIES WHO ROSE FROM THE DEAD

The Hon. Charles Coventry, ex-Etonian, was one of six amateurs who toured with Major Warton's side to South Africa in 1889. At the end of the tour he decided to stay on to join the Bechuanaland Police. Several years later he was involved in the Jameson Raid and a friend reported seeing him stretched out on the ground covered by a blanket: he was therefore presumed dead.

Coventry survived, however, and arrived home unbelievably at the very moment that his own memorial service was taking place at the family chapel in Warwickshire. Coventry was so moved and then delighted by the tributes that were being made that he invited the astonished mourners, some of whom were in a state of considerable shock, to turn the wake into a celebration by having a dance on the village green followed by a banquet. Certainly a novel dance of death.

By a strange coincidence, Coventry's captain on the first tour of South Africa by an official MCC side, C Aubrey Smith, underwent an almost similar experience. Smith had also stayed in the Southern Continent after the tour had finished, to become a stockbroker. After months of intense heat and a time of famine he became very ill. He had contracted typhoid fever caused by the contaminated water supply and also gone down with pleurisy and pneumonia. For a time he had nobody to look after him and lay in bed semi-conscious with only a bottle of liqueur and a tin of Huntley and Palmer's biscuits for company. The *Graaff-Reinet Advertiser* printed the following:

DEATH of MR AUBREY SMITH

Information has been received that Mr Aubrey Smith, who captained the English team during the Cricket Tournament, has succumbed to that fell disease, inflammation of the lungs. For some time past he was confined to his room; but as he took a turn for the better it was thought that he had successfully tided over the crisis. Much regret will be felt at his decease, as during his tour through the Colony and his short stay at the Rand he made many friends by his kindly disposition.

The obituary was nearly 60 years premature.

Eventually Smith was found in a very weakened state and was nursed back to health, later, of course, to return to England and move on to great things on the West End stage and in films in Hollywood. Just after the announcement of his death, an official from the Wanderers Cricket Club had come round to his lodgings to enquire whether the club band could officiate at his funeral. Apparently Smith managed a hollow laugh.

In 1985, veteran cricket commentator Rex Alston read his own obituary in *The Daily Telegraph*. Alston felt that he should let the paper know that far from being cold and stiff he was very warm and supple. Eventually, having been put through on the 'phone to somebody who was aware of what he was talking about, Alston explained that the obituary, though very nice and all that, was a little premature. 'Who is this speaking?' asked the man on the 'phone, somewhat taken aback. 'Rex Alston.' 'Are you sure?' 'Absolutely.' A long pause. And then, in an extremely tremulous voice, 'Where are you speaking from?'

CRICKET GETS CURIOSER AND CURIOSER

So many things can happen at a cricket match and sometimes they actually do.

EXTRAORDINARY OCCURRENCES

In September of 1734, a team apparently disappeared. The press recorded, 'a great cricket match was lately to have been played between the Gentlemen of London and Croydon, but the latter having been regaled with a good dinner etc. *gratis*, withdrew – and have since not been heard of!'

The unexplained departure of the Croydon team after lunch is something of a mystery – perhaps they feasted and imbibed too well and went home to sleep off the effects.

Richard Toomer took umbrage when he was bowled by the legendary David Harris – but not with the bowler. He loaded a gun with shot, fired and successfully hit the ball twelve times in a row.

David Harris, the potter from Odiham, was a feared bowler in the days of Hambledon's cricketing glory. Nyren described the effect of his bowling '. . . woe be to the man who did not get in to block them, for they had such a peculiar ewl, that they would grind his fingers against the bat: many a time have I seen the blood drawn in this way from a batter who was not up to the trick . . .' Harris was not such a great shakes as a batsman and towards the end of his career suffered much from gout. When he batted an armchair was brought to the wicket so that after each ball he was able to 'sit down in his own calm and simple grandeur and repose'.

A curious Cricket Match, 1834
A game of cricket was played at Newenden, Kent, between five

Gentlemen of Kent and five of Sussex which terminated as follows:

Kent	First innings
Mr. J. Tolhurst	0 b by Warner
Mr. T. Ayerst	0 b by Warner
Mr. W. Hunson	0 b by Warner
Mr. R. Levett	0 b by Warner
Mr. S. Maynard	0 leg before wicket

Sussex	First innings
Mr. J. Furner	0 b by Ayerst
Mr. T. Edwards	0 b by Ayerst
Mr. T. Coppinger	0 b by Ayerst
Mr. R. Moore	0 b by Ayerst
Mr. T. Warner	0 b by Ayerst

Night coming on prevented the second innings being played!

In a match between MCC and Ground and the North at Lord's in 1840, Bass and Dakin were batting when a stroke into the outfield reached Captain Liddell who threw

the ball in hard at the wicket. The throw was somewhat misdirected as the ball struck Bass's hat, knocked it off and then vanished from sight. Some time later it was discovered lodged between the lining and the crown of the hat.

The dashing Captain Adamson was so attracted by a lady spectator at a match in Phoenix Park, Dublin that he deserted his position on the boundary to go and converse with her. Fortunately, he was not entirely distracted for as he was springing back over a four foot high spiked fence, he took a brilliant left-handed catch while still in mid-air.

In the first match of R A Fitzgerald's North American tour of 1872 against Montreal, W G Grace had scored 81 in most convincing fashion, when he struck hard towards Mr Benjamin, 'a stout fielder with spectacles on his nose and a pipe in his mouth, who suddenly received the ball in his abdomen, where it lodged and the Champion of England was forced to retire caught'.

Another Grace happening occurred in 1878 at Clifton, Bristol where Gloucestershire were playing Surrey. Grace was running between the wickets when the ball was thrown in and somehow managed to get marooned in his shirt. Pursued by amused fielders, Grace ran six, three with the ball in its temporary lodging before being stopped and asked to give it up. This he refused to do as he suspected that there would be an appeal for 'handling the ball'. There was a fair amount of friendly jostling before the ball was recovered.

Percy de Paravicini, Cambridge blue at the time of the Studd dynasty and a county player for Middlesex as well as a soccer international and winning FA Cup finalist for Old Etonians in 1882, played perhaps two of the most extraordinary successive strokes in organized cricket.

In a club level match he arrived at the wicket with the game in its last minute or so and 15 runs required to win. De Paravicini hit the first ball he received for 8 and the second for 7!

Bow 99 v Chalcot, 27 and 11. In Chalcot's first innings H Payne scored 24 not out and in their second, 10 not out. There were 3 wides in the first innings and one in the second so that the other ten batsmen were each out twice for nought – an extraordinary ten 'pairs' from one side.

In a match between Surrey and Middlesex at the Oval, F C Holland started the match fielding for Surrey – his name had been printed on the scorecards as one of the home team – however, after a number of overs had been bowled Holland, to his obvious surprise, was called off the field and replaced by W S Lees.

During H M Martineau's XI tour of Egypt in 1933, C H Knott scored 191 in a match against Alexandria, the last 91 of which came in roughly a quarter-of-an-hour. The spectacular innings included 15 sixes and 17 fours and was accompanied by a strange wailing noise. Being told that the wailing came from just over the boundary wall seemed to encourage Knott to further efforts. Every time the ball cleared the wall, the wailing increased and it seemed

judicious not to attempt to retrieve the balls. In fact, recovery was not necessary as every ten minutes or so little boys would bring them back onto the ground demanding backsheesh.

Colonel Douglas Brett won a gallantry award when he summarily dispatched armed Hindu terrorists who disrupted a match in which he was playing at Chittagong in India in 1934. As the gang charged onto the pitch Brett became so incensed at having his concentration disturbed that he started to lay into them with his bat. His fire-power was too much for the marauders and they fled in disarray.

Ulyett once hit a ball from Manchester to Bradford in a match between Yorkshire and Lancashire. The ball went through an open carriage window of a passing train and was not recovered until it had reached the station in the Yorkshire wool town. It is said the Great Northern charged porterage for its return.

During a match between Yorkshire and Derbyshire at Dewsbury, someone left the taps running in a room over the Derbyshire dressing-room. The water seeped through the ceiling and ruined most of the players' gear. Two of the side escaped fairly lightly, had spiked shoes and therefore had to bowl when Derbyshire took the field, whereas the rest turned out in lounge suits.

In a match between Tadcaster and Church Fenton, at Church Fenton, the visiting side were short of an umpire and a local man, who was a bowler of some repute, agreed to fill the gap. Early on in the game, a Tadcaster bowler was on the point of appealing for lbw but before he could get the words out the umpire shouted excitedly, 'How's that?' (obviously momentarily forgetting he was not bowling). The Tadcaster trundler looked at him in some surprise. 'I was going to say that. How is it?' 'Not out,' said the umpire.

In a country match in South Africa, Bobby Simpson, the Australian captain, forgot to tell his opposite number that he wished to enforce the follow-on; the lead was nearly 450. The result was that both sides came out to field after the 10 minute interval!

While batting for Brighton against Hawthorn East in a Victoria District match, Test batsman C C McDonald was distracted by a commotion at the boundary. Throwing down his bat he rushed to assist a railway porter who was struggling to detain a youth who was afterwards charged with stealing.

Neil Hawke, the courageous Australian seamer was so angry at being given out lbw in an East Lancashire match that he knocked the stumps over with his bat. Later, full of remorse, he sent a small boy around the ground carrying a blackboard on which he (Hawke) had chalked an apology.

During a tedious match in dull weather between Sussex and Leicestershire, fast bowler John Snow enlivened proceedings by bowling a bouncer with a red soap cricket ball that he had just bought in a local department store. Batsman Peter Marner hooked it ferociously. The ball shattered into countless fragments. The Sussex scorer solemnly noted in his scorebook: 'Ball exploded'.

The most protracted cricket match lasted a mere 20 years. Every year on 4 June, the teams congregated at Avondale Park, Galveston, and played until one wicket fell. They then retired for refreshment, parted and met again exactly one year later. Onto the field they trooped, play resumed, a wicket fell and off they came. Who said the game was nothing but a ritual?

Keith Pont of Essex was getting weary fielding at third man from both ends. At the finish of the next over he grabbed a nearby bicycle and pedalled around the boundary to take up his new position. Undoubtedly, the only player in a first-class match to take a captain's riposte literally: 'On yer bike!'

Ray East, the Essex 2nd XI Coach, was sitting in the dressing-room while his team were batting. The telephone rang and the call was for one of the team who was sauntering around the boundary edge. An urgent waved mime through the dressing-room door seemed sufficient to get the stroller back to the 'phone. East settled back in his chair. Barely a minute or so later the two batsmen who had been at the wicket clumped into the dressing-room.

'Lunch already, lads?' asked East. 'No, we've declared, haven't we,' one replied, 'wasn't that you waving to us?'

Geoff Miller, Derbyshire (now Essex) and England off-spinner, relishes practical jokes. He once hid a 'whoopee' cushion under his sweater before coming out to field and then deflated it as the bowler ran up to bowl . . .

At Wallasey Grammar School, a boy playing in a junior match hoisted a

ball above a two-storey building which, on its descent, fell straight down a chimney to eventually emerge, looking black rather than red, in a downstairs classroom.

Insult was added to injury in a Central Lancashire League match between Walsden and Rochdale. Rochdale batsman, Wilson Hartley, struck Walsden bowler, Peter Green, for a massive six which travelled out of the ground and smashed through an upper window of a house in nearby Strines Street. The ball came to rest on the pillow of a bed – the bed of the bowler, Peter Green.

In 1948, 'Evita' of Argentina extracted revenge for a frosty reception in Britain. The ground of the Buenos Aires Cricket Club – a corner of yet another foreign field for UK expatriates – had a visit one night from Peronists who burned down the club house, tore out the fences and drove bulldozers all over the pitch.

The Indian opening batsman, Krishnamashari Srikkanth was the victim of a cruel hoax in 1984 when answering a 'phone call to someone he thought was Test selector Hanumant Singh. The urgent message was for him to fly to Pakistan immediately to join the team. Having flown the first leg of the journey from Madras to Bombay and inquiring after clearance papers to continue his journey, he found he had been 'taken for a ride'.

ODD FACTS AND FEATS

A match between London and Croydon was played in 1731 at Smitham Bottom near the gibbet.

No quarter was given, the result hung in suspense for a long while and it would be apposite to report that the game was drawn.

During a match at Hambledon in the 18th century, Thomas White came in for two innings with a bat as wide as the wicket. The opposition immediately protested and one of them produced a knife and shaved and hacked the bat down to a reasonable size while White vented his displeasure on all who would listen.

In a match between MCC and the Gentlemen of England at Lord's in 1818, it was decided that Mr R Holden should bowl for the Gents from both ends throughout the game and have ten picked fieldsmen. Mr F Ladbroke was absent during the MCC's second innings, so Mr Holden had to be content with 19 wickets. (The totally unjustifiable and unworthy thought strikes one, that Ladbroke could have been ensuring that punters betting on a clean sweep for Holden would not collect their dividends.)

In a match between England and 22 of Nottingham in 1818, the game is said to have been 'sold' on both sides. One of the umpires was replaced for cheating and Lord Frederick Beauclerk's finger was broken by a fielder on his own side who had become over-anxious because his noble Lordship was bowling too well. The fieldsman, having backed the opposition, could see his stake was going the way of the wickets and so he endeavoured to incapacitate Beauclerk by bowling the ball fiercely at him from a short distance.

At the Gentlemen v Players match at Lord's in 1837, the Players were given a handicap by having to defend wickets comprising four stumps – 36×12 inches. The Gents had the concession of three stumps – 27×8 inches. Even so, the Players won by an innings and 10 runs. The game was referred to as the 'Barn Door Match'.

A single-wicket match in 1853 was played between Mr Barrett and Mr Swain. Swain was credited with 5 and Barrett 3 and then 1. Quiz question: How was it that neither batsman scored a run? Answer: They were all wides!

Thomas Wentworth Spencer Wills was an extraordinarily adventurous, diverse and persuasive character. He played for Cambridge against Oxford in 1856, though he was not a student in residence, and he practised as a solicitor in Brisbane in 1860 though he never qualified to do so. He was born on the Molonglo

Plains in New South Wales and was sometimes a fast round-arm bowler and sometimes a slow under-arm bowler. He played for his school, Rugby, the Gentlemen of Kent and over a twenty-year period in sixteen matches for Victoria.

Wills was the first person to teach cricket to the aborigines (on his father's sheep stations) and on one occasion travelled 1,800 miles to play in a game. Wills' mother lived to the age of 92, his father and brothers were murdered by natives while on exploration trips in Australia, and after developing alcoholic problems he finished his own life as he had lived it, colourfully, by stabbing himself to death at Heidelberg, in May 1880.

During the 1850s, a New York millionaire, Hesketh K Naylor, who, apparently, was impotent, kept an establishment of women with fuller figures to play cricket with balloons in the nude. Naylor apparently derived sexual gratification from watching them score although he did not do so himself. A record of the matches has been discreetly mislaid.

F S Spofforth, the 'Demon' bowler, mastered the knack of throwing a new-laid egg a distance of over 50 yards without it breaking when it came to land.

The Hon F S Jackson, who when at Harrow had Winston Churchill as his fag, achieved a feat surely without parallel when he made 3 centuries in 4 successive innings spread over four seasons in one of which he did not play at all. In 1899, he made a century in his last innings, he played once in 1900 and made a century in his second innings and then his next

appearance was not until 1902 when he made a century in his first innings.

Eustace Shine obviously did not rub the ball hard enough while bowling for Kent against Surrey at the Oval in 1897. He got 'clobbered' for 226 runs. Shine was largely instrumental in getting the compulsory follow-on law changed to being optional. Playing for Cambridge in the University match 1896, he deliberately bowled 3 balls – 2 of them no-balls – aimed at the boundary to help accumulate the necessary runs in order to prevent Oxford following-on.

E J Diver was the first of the few cricketers to turn out for both the Gentlemen and the Players. As an amateur he played for Surrey and taught at Wimbledon College. As a professional he played for Warwickshire and became a publican. During his time with Warwickshire, Diver played in 118 first-class matches. In his second match, against Nottinghamshire at Trent Bridge, he took 6 for 58. After that, he never took another wicket for the county.

It is reported that George Gunn once scored 777 in a single-wicket game.

Major Booth, promising Yorkshire all-rounder, who, despite his Christian name, never exceeded the rank of 2nd Lieutenant, lost his life in France during the First World War. His distraught sister refused to believe of his death and kept a candle lit in his room, which remained untouched exactly as he had left it, awaiting his return. This state of affairs continued until her own death in 1950.

Cricket has more than its share of fanatics. Some of them believe that in Paradise they will still be able to play the game on Elysian fields. Harry Bagshaw, the Derbyshire umpire, made sure that not only would he be properly dressed but that he would be fully prepared when the new ball was needed. When interred, Bagshaw was wearing his umpire's coat and clutching a cricket ball. The tombstone depicted broken stumps,

dislodged bails and an umpire's hand with index finger raised skywards, signalling 'Out'.

The only cricket match ever to be staged at an Olympic Games took place at the Paris Olympics in 1900. Devon County Wanderers represented Britain and they beat the Athletic Club of Paris, representing France, by 158 runs at the Vélodrome de Vincennes. The Wanderers team, who now no longer exist as such, was a combination of players from Old Blundellians and Castle Cary. In July 1987 a celebratory return match took place at Meudon. On

this occasion Old Blundellians and Standard Athletic Club drew.

A J Atfield (Gloucestershire and Wiltshire) married in June 1903 at St George's, Hanover Square in London and then proceeded to score a century before lunch for Cross Arrows in a match at Lord's on the same day.

Charles Newhall, of the once famous Philadelphia Eleven, always went into bat carrying a lemon not only to suck before each stroke, but also to enable him to spit into the wicket keeper's eye if the latter appealed too loudly for a dismissal.

George Beet, later a well-known umpire, was a dependable wicket-keeper for Derbyshire before and after the First World War. In the same side for several seasons was fast bowler Fred Root. Many score-cards were thus embellished: Beet-root!

W H Foulkes played for Derbyshire and kept goal for Sheffield United, Chelsea and England, and at one time weighed over 21 stone – one of the heaviest cricketers ever. After his career was over, he 'earned a crust' on Blackpool Sands soliciting the public to take penalty kicks which he attempted to save.

Nonagenarian Donald Adams played only one first-class match in his life – for Surrey against London County in 1902 at Crystal Palace. He obtained one wicket – that of W G Grace.

Gerald de Lisle Hough played a couple of seasons for Kent in the immediate post-World War I years. A war wound impeded his bowling ability and in first-class cricket he took only one wicket – that was with the first ball he bowled.

R T Stanyforth had the unusual distinction of captaining England on the 1927/8 tour of South Africa without having appeared in first-class County cricket.

R A Young, Cambridge University, Sussex and England – also an amateur soccer international, one game against Hungary – maintained that any fielding captain should have the right to pour up to 100 gallons of water onto the pitch.

J R Gill made a century in his only first-class match. Gill scored 106 for Gentlemen of Ireland against MCC at Dublin in 1948. He opened the batting and then in the second innings was out for a duck.

Malcolm Nash, Glamorgan left-arm seamer, has put forward the view that visiting captains should always win the toss in order to nullify the advantage of pitches specially prepared for 'home' bowlers.

Two sets of Bedser twins have played cricket. No introduction is needed for the Berkshire pair, Alec and Eric; their namesakes

Cornhill Team Award
Winner of each Match £5,000

Cornhill Player Awards
Player of the Series   £1,000
Player of each Match   £500

England v. West Indies

18p

AT HEADINGLEY
Third Test Match

Thursday, Friday, Saturday, Monday & Tuesday. 12th, 13th, 14th, 16th & 17th July, 1984

18p

ENGLAND

First Innings :   Second Innings :

1—C. G. Greenidge ....
2—D. L. Haynes ....
3—I. V. A. Richards .. ..
4—H. A. Gomes ....
*5—C. H. Lloyd ....
†6—P. J. Dujon ....
7—M. D. Marshall ....
8—M. A. Holding ....
9—J. Garner ....
10—E. A. Baptiste ....
11—R. A. Harper ....

Extras   .. ..   Extras ....
Total ....   Total ....

FALL OF WICKETS :—

First Innings :
Second Innings :

Bowlers	Overs	Mdns.	Runs	Wkts.	Bowlers	Overs	Mdns.	Runs	Wkts.
Garner									
Marshall									

* Denotes Captain   † Denotes Wicket Keeper

Umpires : D. J. Constant and D. L. Evans
Scorers : E. I. Lester and A. E. Weld

WEST INDIES

First Innings :   Second Innings :

1—G. Fowler ....
2—B. C. Broad ....
3—V. P. Terry ....
4—G. J. Lamb ....
*5—D. I. Gower ....
6—I. T. Botham ....
†7—P. R. Downton ....
8—D. R. Pringle ....
9—N. G. B. Cook ....
10—R. G. D. Willis ....
11—N. G. Cowans Allott ....

Extras   ....   Extras ....
Total ....   Total ....

FALL OF WICKETS :—

First Innings :
Second Innings :

Bowlers	Overs	Mdns.	Runs	Wkts.	Bowlers	Overs	Mdns.	Runs	Wkts.

Hours of Play : Thursday to Monday, 11.00 a.m. to 6.00 p.m.
Tuesday, 11.00 a.m. to 5.30 p.m. or 6.00 p.m.

Lunch : 1.00 p.m. to 1.40 p.m.
Tee : 3.40 p.m. to 4.00 p.m.

ADJUDICATOR : CORNHILL Player of the Match — A. R. LEWIS
Player of the Match —

---

christened after them performed in South Africa. Both were all-round sportsmen and Alec, who was killed aged 33 in a car accident in Johannesburg in 1981, was a medium-paced seamer who turned out for Border in the Currie Cup in 1971–72. An earlier car accident had effectively curtailed his cricketing career.

A batsman called Grove was caught off the first ball of a Western Australian Grade match at Melvista Oval in the mid-1960s. However, the umpire recalled him to the wicket having ruled that no signal had been given for the game to begin.

For those with 'blind' faith in the printed word, the greatest number of 'foreign bodies' appearing for any side apparently occurred at Headingley in 1984 on the first day of the third Test between England and the West Indies. The scorecard

showed all the Caribbean players appearing for the 'old country' and *vice versa*. The sheet was quickly withdrawn and a revised one issued. The price, too, was revised – from 18p to 25p.

The scorebook from a recent match in Essex reads:
S Ansarel c Laurel b Hardy 0.

A well-known local cricketer in Northern Ireland was fired at as he was rolling the pitch for his club in 1969. The shot missed and the game was cancelled.

Ron Yeomans, Yorkshire cricket fanatic, laid bits of turf from nearly two dozen major cricket grounds in his back garden. Apparently, Fenner's provided the best turf and the Oval the worst.

Younis Ahmed was dismissed by Worcestershire for betting against his own county in a John Player League match.

An unusual feature of the cricket ground at a Market Harborough/ Lutterworth needle match at the turn of the century was a water pump situated 10 yds inside the boundary. A Lutterworth player had bet an opponent £10 that his side would win and after they had made a substantial score it seemed likely he would collect his winnings. Harborough then went in and were doing badly until a batsman hit the ball right into the spout of the water pump. All the fielders in turn tried desperately to release the ball but to no avail. An appeal for 'lost ball' was rejected on the grounds that it could be seen. By the time a plumber with a hacksaw was found to free the ball the score had mounted by well over 100 runs and Market Harborough ran out comfortable winners. The Lutterworth player then refused to pay up which led his aggrieved fellow-punter to write to the MCC for a ruling. Eventually a reply was forthcoming confirming the umpire's verdict but recommending that for future games the spout be turned away from the wicket.

GAMES IN UNUSUAL AND DIFFICULT CIRCUMSTANCES

Cricket has been played many times with physical, material and geographical handicaps. There have been games played during earthquakes and enemy action, in the Arctic Circle, at the South Pole, in the middle of the desert, in jungle clearings and up mountain passes, on horseback, on bicycles, on frozen lakes and in Windsor Great Park under moonlight. It has also suffered interruptions from trains and boats and 'planes. Some details of other instances are duly noted: During the well-documented match between Greenwich Pensioners possessing only one leg and those with only one arm, which was 'so much in favour of the Timber-toes, as never to be recovered by the dint of Arms', it was reported there were five broken legs. Providentially, they were all wooden.

A thought-provoking instance of how cricket can be played by the disabled is evident in a cutting from the *Westmoreland Gazette* describing a club game: 'One of the most remarkable features was the playing of Walker, a youth from Burneside, without hands, having been unfortunately deprived of those useful members by an accident at the paper mill. Maimed as he is, he can do anything in the game except bowl. He bats very tolerably, and certainly most extraordinarily for his means; catches a ball upon his chest, with the assistance of his arms; and throws up a ball with remarkable precision by means of his foot.'

In 1776, cricket was played on skates on ice in Poplar Neck. Poplar outskated Wapping in no uncertain manner.

The Mere Fen near Cambridge became frozen in the winter of 1870, enabling a combined England and Cambridge University XI to risk their reputations as well as limbs by taking on 16 of the neighbourhood of Suravesey on ice. The Combined team won easily enough but not before suffering severe bruising when losing their equilibrium.

'A game between Surrey and Lancashire at the Oval was suspended for one hour because of the intense heat in July 1868.'

Circus cricket was played in Johannesburg during the first tour by an English side, 1889/90. The South African 'Blondin', as Professor Cogan described himself, conducted a match from the high wire against four members of the Wanderers

Club at the Club ground. Two poles were placed a pitch-length apart and suspended between them was a slack wire on which the intrepid 'Prof' stood. The wicket was hung from one end of the wire. Cogan managed to score 69 runs before he was bowled. He, in turn, then bowled from the wire against the four who, needless to say, batted at ground level and who were handicapped by having to use a pick-handle instead of the willow. Between them, they accumulated 113.

'Buns' Thornton, playing for Scarborough Visitors against Malton in Yorkshire managed to get a fielder into deep water. There was a pond in one corner of the ground and the opposing captain, realizing that such a tempting target would be bound to attract an intuitive hitter like Thornton, placed a man beyond the pond to take a likely catch. Sure enough, Thornton soon lofted a drive into the middle of the pond and the unfortunate fielder with eyes only for the ball, fell right in.

The perils of playing games of cricket on Goodwin Sands were never more obvious than during one match when the stumps were sucked under by quicksand.

A game of cricket was played on top of a two-million gallon oil tank at Adelaide in 1940. The playing area was over 100 ft wide.

In July 1944, during a game between Army and Royal Air Force at Lord's, a flying-bomb apparently heading for the ground caused both players and spectators to take 'evasive action' by lying flat on the ground. Captain J D Robertson was batting at the time and, the danger having passed and the game resumed, he 'retaliated' immediately by hitting a 6.

Major E W Swanton, RA gave a graphic description in the 1946 *Wisden* of Cricket under the Japs. He recalled that the 'first of the camps on the Thai–Burma railway on which we played cricket was Wampo. Christmas Day, 1942 . . . This particular game was notable

. . . for what is probably the fastest hundred of all time. It was scored in about five overs by a very promising young Eurasian cricketer called Thoy, who, with graceful ease, kept hitting the tennis ball clear over the huts.'

Roger Coates is one of the few, if not the only person to have scored a century in an official match in the small hours of the night. Cambridge Undergraduates mounted a 24-hour cricket match on Parker's Piece in 1973 and Coates' turn for a knock arrived at nearly a quarter-to-two in the morning. With the help of good eyesight, two gas arc lights, four street lamps and a full moon he proceeded stealthily towards a nocturnal hundred.

THE SPOKEN WORD

TALES WITH TAGS

The minute book of the old Hambledon Club revealed that on convivial evenings the players regularly raised their glasses to toast 'Madge'. 'Who was Madge?' subsequent generations have asked. 'Was she the barmaid?' 'Or perhaps a well-known lady hiding her identity?' It took a curator of the MCC – a lady herself – to ferret out the mystery, revealed in the pages of Grose's *Dictionary of the Vulgar Tongue*. 'Madge' was 18th century 'slang' for the private parts of a woman.

Edward Pooley, one of the greatest wicket-keepers of his day, loved to gamble, and while in New Zealand was tempted to make a quick 'buck'.

The England side were playing a series of games in which the opposition numbered 22 and at one of them Pooley struck a bet with a spectator called Ralph Donkin at odds of £1 to a shilling that he could correctly forecast each batsman's total. Knowing that the local cricketers were very inexperienced, Pooley predicted 'ducks' for the whole team and was proved half-right when 11 failed to score. He then demanded the money he'd won but Donkin refused to pay up, saying it had been a trick. This led to a spectacular brawl and Pooley was arrested and charged with personal assault and damage to property.

The English side had to play the rest of the tour without their number one wicket-keeper and Harry Jupp, the deputy, known as 'Young Stonewall', suffered from eye inflammation as well as a bout of insanity and missed several matches. It was not until after they had returned home that Pooley eventually left New Zealand having been found not guilty. The New Zealand public thought him badly treated and raised a subscription as well as presenting him with a gold ring.

Pooley spent the last years of his life in the workhouse at Lambeth crippled by arthritis and rheumatism. To a journalist who interviewed him at that time, he said with bitter realism, 'It was the workhouse, sir, or the river.'

A E Knight, Leicestershire and England and author of *The Complete Cricketer*, could be said to have been a disciple of 'muscular Christianity' His practice of going down on his knees at the crease before each innings to pray for heavenly help did not amuse the cantankerous Lancashire fast bowler Walter Brearley. Brearley voiced a complaint to the umpire that he thought Knight was receiving unfair assistance.

Jack Newman of Hampshire once appealed against the light and was turned down. Showing signs of dissent at the umpire's decision he was rebuked by his batting partner, his captain, the Hon. Lionel Tennyson, from the other end of the pitch. Seeing that Newman was cocking a so-called 'deaf-un' to his remonstrations, Tennyson shouted in annoyance 'Can you hear me, Newman?' A reply was immediately forthcoming. 'Yes, my Lord, but where are you speaking from?'

A N Hornby, dashing Lancashire and England batsman, was nicknamed 'Monkey' because of his small physique. He was one of the team that Lord Harris took to Australia in 1878/79. On the Sydney cricket ground Hornby 'arrested' a spectator who, annoyed at an umpiring decision, had rushed onto the field and struck his Lordship with a stick. Hornby successfully 'frogmarched his prisoner' to the pavilion despite being hit in the face and having his shirt nearly torn off his back.

A year or so later Hornby was playing in the Gentlemen and Players match at the Oval, and with W G Grace had been batting well until he lofted a powerful drive and was brilliantly caught in the outfield by William Gunn who stood 6 ft 3 in in his socks.

'Bad luck, Monkey,' said the incoming batsman to the disconsolate Hornby. 'Yes,' replied Hornby, 'no one but a damned giraffe would have got near it.'

The fiery Charles Kortright was undoubtedly the victor in a clash with W G Grace at a match between Essex and Gloucestershire at Leyton in 1898. On the first day of the game Grace had extracted considerable revenge for being refused admission to the ground by the Essex gateman – it would seem that Grace had the wrong pass and the gateman was applying strictly the letter of the law – by capturing 7 wickets and then scoring a century. However, in the Gloucestershire second innings Kortright brought Essex back into the contest by proceeding to bowl at his quickest pace. Having dismissed two batsmen for ducks he then triumphantly appealed for a glaringly obvious caught and bowled against Grace. A thunderous frown from the great man persuaded the umpire to respond with 'not out'. There were further appeals from Kortright when bowling to Grace later in his innings, one for what seemed plumb lbw and also a catch behind the wicket. They were similarly rejected. Finally, Kortright fired in a totally unplayable delivery. The middle and leg stumps were uprooted and after lengthy hesitation, Grace could think of no alternative but to walk. 'Surely you're not going, Doc,' said Kortright with mock surprise, 'there's still one stump standing.'

Johnny Douglas had a reputation for being a resolute though unimaginative captain of Essex. In one match in which the county were being given a deal of leather hunting he displayed an obvious lack of vision.

Douglas was bowling himself and decided to put on Claude Ashton – never more than an occasional bowler – at the other end to try and stem the flow of runs. The opposition took an immediate liking to Ashton's innocuous deliveries and the score mounted rapidly. Everyone expected Ashton to be withdrawn from the attack, but Douglas was so wrapped up in his own efforts that he allowed the situation to continue until his fellow bowler had been feeding 'fodder' to the batsmen for well over an hour. Eventually Ashton's elder brother, Hubert, approached the captain and tactfully suggested that young Claude might well be rested. 'Christ,' said Douglas, 'is he still bowling?'

In 1922 Tennyson, became one of the few skippers to send a player from the field (Lord Hawke and Brian Bolus were two others). The belligerent Newman had kicked over the stumps in annoyance at a decision during a match at Trent Bridge and so was dismissed peremptorily from the scene of action. Later, after a good 'talking-to', Newman apologized and was rewarded with a pound note from Tennyson.

Philip Mead had a reputation for inadvertently running out batting partners. One day his Hants colleague, Johnny Arnold, decided to exact reprisal. As he and Mead were crossing in the middle of a run, Arnold struck his bat between the great man's legs which sent him sprawling on all fours, desperately trying to regain his balance. Arnold stopped running and began to laugh uproariously. Mead had the last laugh. Arnold was so busy relishing Mead's misfortune that he failed to notice he himself had been run out.

The genial and expansive Maharajah of Porbander, who captained the Indian touring side to Britain in 1932, was appointed more for reasons of social distinction than playing ability. The Maharajah brought with him a fleet of white Rolls-Royces and different vehicles were always at hand to transport His Highness from station to hotel to ground, wherever he might happen to be.

At the end of the tour, one unkind critic pointed out that Porbander had more Rolls-Royces in his possession than runs in the scorebook.

At the Hampshire and Nottinghamshire match at Portsmouth in 1968 a warning for one of the spectators was broadcast over the tannoy: 'Don't eat the sausage sandwiches – the sausages are off.' The recipient of this message from his parents was a boy, Paul Brown, who was then invited over the loudspeaker to lunch in the members room at Hampshire Club's expense.

Ray East, knowing left-arm spinner and improvisatory right-hand batsman for Essex, was and is a renowned humorist. On one occasion he walked out to bat against fast bowler Shuttleworth of Lancashire on a fiery pitch and did not fancy his chances of avoiding being hit on some part of his anatomy. So, in passing the bowler on the way to the wicket, East whispered encouragingly that if he (Shuttleworth) could see his way to pitch the next delivery up and keep it straight the bat would not impede the progress of the ball on its way to the stumps. East could then retire gracefully to the pavilion bodily intact. Shuttleworth duly obliged, bowled a half-volley on middle and leg and East responded with a mighty swing which was meant to

miss the ball. To Shuttleworth's fury and East's pretended alarm the swing did not miss the ball – in fact, it sent it many a yard over the distant boundary for six.

Shuttleworth's remarks were less than comradely. As he stormed in to bowl the next ball, East decided to take evasive action. He threw away his bat, dived to the ground and lay flat on his stomach with his hands on his head. The bouncer flew harmlessly by.

At the end of the Cornhill series against New Zealand in 1983, umpire 'Dicky' Bird was presented with a commemorative medal within its box. At least, it appeared that that was the case. In fact, it was only the case that Bird had, for when he opened the lid, he found that inside there was – no medal. New Zealand bowler, Ewen Chatfield, who was an onlooker, immediately gave the signal for 'one short'.

QUOTES

William Wilberforce, the great emancipator, wrote a letter to his friend, Lord Muscaster, in 1810, in which he complained, 'playing cricket with Mr Babington, a ball struck my foot with great violence and by the positive injunctions of my surgeon I have ever since been sentenced to a sofa'.

The celebrated John Wisden was a member of the first touring side to leave these shores for the USA and Canada in 1859. Leaving Liverpool, it was not long before the sea became extremely rough. Suffering from severe nausea Wisden groaned that what the ocean needed was 'the immediate use of the roller'.

The great Ranji inspired Edwardian journalists to purple prose. They described his demeanour on the field as having 'an Oriental calm with an Occidental quickness, the stillness of a panther with the suddenness of its spring'. His beautifully refined leg-glance had been honed to perfection during his apprenticeship at Cambridge Unviersity, when he had stoically endured the handicap imposed by his coach of having his right leg pegged to the ground. The stroke gave the impression 'almost as if he had struck a match on the ball as it went by'.

Dr E M Grace, brother of the legendary W G, was a coroner by profession and unquestionably a man who had his priorities in the right place. On one occasion when playing in a game many miles from his Gloucestershire home, a telegram arrived urgently requesting his appearance at an inquest. The coroner wired back: 'Impossible to come today. Please put corpse on ice.'

Ernie Jones, Australian tearaway who bounced a ball through W G Grace's beard, was asked by the Prince of Wales if he had gone to Adelaide's Prince Alfred College. 'Yeah,' replied Jones, 'I drove the dust-cart there.'

The immortal Wilfred Rhodes, who tragically became a victim of blindness in later life, was known for his keen eyesight during his playing days. Someone asked him once: 'Is it true, Wilfred, that after you had been batting for a while, you could see the seam on the ball?' The reply was succinct: 'Ay, that's right, lad. But tha' should 'ave played with Ranji; he could see the stitches.'

Once, when Kent wanted 218 to win against the clock, the opening batsmen were Frank Woolley and Bill Ashdown. The score mounted rapidly with Woolley striking superbly. At the end of an over, Ashdown went down the pitch to have a word with his partner. 'Don't hit so many sixes. It wastes too much time.'

Gerry Weighall, Kent cricketer, described the omission of Frank Woolley from the England side on one occasion: 'the greatest crime since the Crucifixion'.

Charlie Harris, Notts opening batsman for many years, was renowned for a dry sense of humour. On arriving at the wicket at the start of the day's play, he would address the fielding side: 'Good morning, fellow workers'.

Arthur Mailey, Australian leg-break bowler, talented writer and cartoonist, used to relate a story of being invited to a ball at a country house. His aristocratic hostess, who knew absolutely nothing about cricket, became bored with his conversation.

'Aren't you going to dance, Mr Mailey?' she enquired querulously.

'No, ma'am, I'm a little stiff from bowling.'

'Oh, really,' she replied, 'so that's where you come from.'

Australia's PM Bob Hawke was no mean wicket-keeper/batsman. A first grade player in Western Australia, he was sometimes co-opted as 12th man for the University side at Oxford. A new drink, Kummel, was being promoted at one game in which Hawke played and he took a liberal attitude towards its consumption, even though he usually espoused a different political flavour. The salutory effect was his dismissal, first ball.

As he returned dejectedly to the pavilion, the scorer called out: 'Bowler's name?'

From the fielding skipper came the reply: 'Kummel!'

In 1968, Field-Marshal Montgomery strutted into the Australian tourists' dressing-room at Southampton and asked: 'Were any of you chaps with me in the Desert?'

'To me a fast bowler is like an animal. If he smells fear he will be after you twice as hard.' (Ian Chappell)

'To go to a cricket match for nothing but cricket is as though a man were to go into an inn for nothing but drink.' (Neville Cardus)

Arlott commentary: 'The fieldsmen are scattered in the wilderness like missionaries.' He also once described MCC members as having 'their ants full of pants'.

It is not only many spectators who abhor the modern practice of hugging and kissing at the fall of every wicket. Maurice Hallam, who was usually an infallible slip fielder for Leicestershire, dropped an easy chance off the bowling of his captain early one morning. Asked why it had happened, Hallam replied: 'I couldn't bear being kissed by Tony Lock at this hour of the day'.

Sidney Barnes, abrasive Aussie opening batsman, never missed an opportunity to have a joke at the expense of authority. During the 1948 tour of England, umpire Alec Skelding turned down an appeal that Barnes thought was valid. At that moment a dog ran onto the outfield, so Barnes ran, picked up the animal and took it to Skelding. As he put the dog at the umpire's feet, he remarked: 'Now all you need is a white stick.'

A Jamaican judge in Kingston High Court suddenly announced: 'I have to tell you, gentlemen, that Boyce is dismissed'.

'But, m'lud,' queried the defence counsel plaintively, 'my client's name is Bryce.'

'Ah, quite so,' said his lordship, 'but I thought you would like to know the latest Test score from Sabina Park.'

Robin Marlar is renowned for the telling comment in *The Sunday Times*. Referring to Ian Botham's inflamed tendon in 1984, he wrote: 'He will bowl more comfortably after all the fragments of bone and gristle have been vacuumed out of the joint – no, not that kind, silly.' During the summer of 1987, when analysing the form of the England team, Marlar observed that when 'bad luck attaches itself to a team, it clings like a cloak to a highwayman'.

Richard Hadlee was once described by Peter Roebuck in *The Cricketer* as having, 'the appearance of a rickety church steeple and a severe manner which suggests that women are not likely to be ordained just yet'.

Keith Fletcher to Peter Roebuck with a sally worthy of the recent Pakistan tour: "'Ere, Rupert, you've got to 'it the ball to be lbw in this game. If you miss it, you can only be caught!'

'This fellow is the most overrated player I've seen. He looks too heavy, and the way he's been bowling out here, he wouldn't burst a paper bag.' (Harold Larwood, commenting on Ian Botham in *Sunday People*, Australia recorded in *WCM*)

During the recent World Cup, Martin Johnson in The Independent *newspaper wrote that the fast bowler Courtney Walsh, 'who has effectively lost West Indies both their matches, was presented with a carpet for not running out Salim Jaffer off the final ball. He was last seen trying to fly home on it.'*

'When you come back from touring Australia you almost feel like you've been in Vietnam.' (Glenn Turner, *WCM*)

Len Hutton of David Gower: 'He makes batting look as easy as drinking tea.'

The 3rd Test at Eden Gardens, Calcutta, between India and the West Indies ended on New Year's Day, 1988, as a somnolent draw. Dilip Rao in *The Guardian* found that sitting through the match 'was as exciting as watching ivy climb a wall'.

Ex-Foreign Office minister Sir Ian Gilmour on the proposed Poll Tax: 'It is as fair as Pakistani cricket umpire, Shakoor Rana'. (*The Sun*)

The cricketers of Dulwich found an apt description to express their feelings about leaderine Thatcher. One end of their playing area adjoins the high security enclave where "'er indoors' has a home. It is known, appropriately, as 'the cow shed end'.' (*The Guardian*)

GOING, GOING, GONE

Cricket auctions have occurred with ever increasing frequency in the last decade. Phillips, Christie's, less often Sotheby's and Bonhams have all mounted sales – some spectacular that tend to leave the collecting fraternity shaking their heads wondering when the upward spiral of prices is going to even out. Previous generations saw large collections disperse under the auctioneer's hammer far less regularly; some notable occasions in the past have been the sale of the cricket books of the 'Old Buffer', Frederick Gale, at the end of the last century, writer R S Holmes's collection in 1933, that of E W Shepherd in 1954 and the doyen acquirer of cricketing trove, J W Goldman in 1966. There was such a rich variety of desirable items at Goldman's sale that many lots failed to meet their reserve. At Hodgson's sale of Shepherd's books a complete set of *Wisden's Almanacks* went for £145. This same set, updated to 1969, was again auctioned by Hodgson's in 1972 and realized £480. Since then:

April 1979: A set lacking 9 issues sold at Phillips – £4,200

May 1980: 'Plum' Warner's set (up to 1963) at Phillips – £7,800

May 1983:
Individual prices
1865 – £520 – Phillips
1867 – £540   „
1875 – £340   „
1877 – £300   „
1878 – £300   „
1879 – £280   „
a run from 1879–1982 – £3,000

November 1983:
1864 (1st issue) £900 – Phillips
a run from 1879–1972 – £4,800
a run from 1880–1984 – £3,200

November 1985: a full run with some photostat replacement pages – £7,800 – Phillips (bought by The Fine Art Society). An 1865 copy stolen during previews.

June 1986:
1864 and 1865 – £6,133 – Phillips (incl. premium and VAT)
1866 –   £725 – Phillips
1869 –   £669   „
1875 – £1,784   „
run from 1864–1985 – £16,669 (122 volumes in 22 consecutive lots)
run from 1864–1984 – £10,258 (bought by J W McKenzie)

November 1987: a complete run £10,500 – Bonham's (bought by J W McKenzie)

This last run is a record price paid for a set in one lot; with buyer's premium and VAT the total price was in the region of £12,000.

The two largest sales have been Phillip's auction of A E Winder's collection (some of which originally belonged to John Arlott) in November 1985 which was spread over two days and was dubbed 'The Sale of the Century', and Christie's auction at Lord's in 1987 of some of the MCC reserve collection, which lasted 11½ hrs and was dubbed 'The Sale of the Double Century'. Some choice items at the Phillip's sale were:

Harrop's chromolithograph of
    English and Australian
    cricketers   £646

Felix's lithograph of The
Eleven of England £1,450
70 bound Vanity Fair prints £1,895
'Bonnor' by Ape £3,010
'Spofforth' by Spy £2,453
A run of the *American
Cricketer* £500 plus
Britcher's Grand Matches
of Cricket, 1795 £758
Fred Lillywhite's Guides –
complete run £1,784

The total bid was £105,414 which
was not, of course, the gross.

At the Bicentenary Sale, where there
was a greater emphasis on
cricketana as opposed to books,
prices rocketed even further:

J W T Manuel caricature of
W G Grace £1,115
  (incl. premium and VAT)
English School watercolour
of *Girls and Boys Holding
Bats* £3,122
Eleanor Hughes D'Eath
portrait of Lewis Cage £11,150
145 Autographed postcards
of early 20th century
cricketers £5,798
Handbill for 1852 match:
One Arm v One Leg Greenwich
Pensioners £557
Belt and gilt clasp with cricket
designs £1,449

*Fifteen biscuitware models of
Victorian cricketers, comprising
2 batsmen, 11 fieldsmen and 2
umpires of the kind used for
cake decoration, were sold for
three times their estimate at a
sale in Droitwich in July 1981.
A Warwickshire dealer bought
the collection for £210 on
behalf of a friend who
apparently was prepared to bid
up to £800.*

c 1785 linen handkerchief
showing cricket at White
Conduit Club £7,805
Mid-18th century oak bat £5,575
Replica of 'The Ashes' urn £150

The total 'take' including premium
and VAT was £328,396; not bad for
what the Chairman of MCC's Arts
and Library Committee described as
'an attractive rag-bag of oddments
from the pavilion basement'. A long
way indeed from the bargain
basement price for a complete set of
Cricket, auctioned at Lady Cahn's
sale in 1951. The lucky buyer paid –
£1.

CRICKET AND THE PUB

The two are totally synonymous.
Test match stadia, County grounds
and village greens all have a tavern
within a hoick for six. Games are
planned, plots hatched and scores
settled over a glass or two or three
in a pub. Ever since the days of the
Bat and Ball on Broadhalfpenny
and even before, cricketers have
used the local inn as a kind of
pavilion extension. There is record

of a pub named **The Cricket Players**
kept by Oliver Buck at Barker's
Gate, Nottingham as early as 1799
and one called the **Sign of the Hit
or Miss** in Chatham at about the
same time. We know also that
Charles Dickens allowed William
Stocker Trood (adapted to Edwin
Drood for his last unfinished novel),
landlord of the **Sir John Falstaff
Inn** and Treasurer of the Higham

Club, to open a drinking-booth at his home, Gad's Hill, for the Charity matches. The list of pubs called 'The Cricketers' or 'The Cricketers Arms' is endless, practically every county has a clutch of examples. In recent years, Geoff Wellsteed, has devoted considerable time to searching for names of inns with a cricketing connotation:

The Kestor Inn on Dartmoor. The pub sign depicts a cricketing scene and includes the words 'Headquarters of M.C.C.'. This, in fact, is not the revered and august body of London NW8 but the local village side, Manaton CC who hold their meetings in convivial surroundings.

The Thomas Lord Inn, West Meon, Hants, is decorated with cricket relics. Lord is buried in the nearby churchyard.

The Australian, Lennox Gardens, Milner St., London SW3. Adjacent to where Prince's Cricket Ground was once situated.

Black Bull Inn, Grimston, Leics. Contains exhibition of cricketana – framed portraits, score-cards, commemorative plates, Garfield Sobers' blazer and one of Dennis Lillee's sweatbands.

The Centurion at Barton-on-Sea, Hants. Sign shows Philip Mead, the old Hampshire cricketer, acknowledging a century.

The Cricketers, Duncton, nr. Petworth. Features James Dean, 'The Sussex Ploughboy', 19th century player.

The Cricketers at Lower Green, Southwick, Sussex, is close to the churchyard where John 'Jumper' Juniper, the Sussex left-arm fast bowler is buried. Juniper used to wear a shade over one eye and had enormous feet.

The Cricketers, Brinscall, Lancashire. Clive Lloyd depicted on the pub sign.

Other pubs include:
The Double Century, Slough, Berks.
Maiden Over, Earley, Berks.
Jolly Cricketers, Seer Green, Bucks.
Hobbs Pavilion, Parkers Piece, Cambs.
Kentish Cricketer, Canterbury, Kent.
Long Stop, Leicester, Leics.
Merry Cricketers, London SE8
Royal Cricketers, Old Ford, London E2
Dr W G Grace, London SE20
Twelfth Man, Greasby, Merseyside
Bat and Wickets, Northampton
Yorker, Nottingham
Sticky Wicket, Redditch, Worcs.
Fiery Fred, Sheffield (picture of Trueman bowling)
Larwood and Voce Tavern, Trent Bridge, Nottingham
Test Match, West Bridgford, Notts.
The Leg Trap, Adelaide, Australia
The Stumps, Tenerife, Canary Islands
Split Willow, Llanfairfechan, North Wales.

Two pubs on opposite sides of the road, **The Lamb** and **The Wolf** at Norwood Green, Southall, Middlesex, used to have sides that played each other annually. The winning pub had the kudos of displaying a huge wooden bat on the outside wall for all to see.

CRICKET AND CREATURES GREAT AND SMALL

Animals have often influenced the course of cricket matches, sometimes perhaps with an assertion of territorial rights, inadvertent intervention, pure mischievousness, or simply to show humans that they can beat them at their own game:

FROM CAT TO RAT

A cat called Peter, who inhabited the environs of Lord's for 12 of his 14 years and was a dedicated watcher of the game, found a place in the obituary column of *Wisden*: Peter Cat, whose ninth life ended on 5 November, 1964 (*perhaps the fireworks were too much for him*) . . . preferred a close-up view of the proceedings and his sleek, black form could often be seen prowling on the field of play when the crowds were biggest. He frequently appeared on the television screen. Mr S C Griffith, Secretary of MCC, said of him: 'He was a cat of great character and loved publicity.'

On Harefield Common in 1827 a well-publicized game of novelty cricket was played. Two gentlemen of Middlesex had challenged a local farmer, Francis Trumper, and his thoroughbred sheep dog for a considerable stake. In the first innings the two gents managed to score 3 between them and Trumper and dog accumulated 5. At this stage the odds of 5 to 1 against the farmer and his canine companion had been hedged to the extent that

they were nearly reversed. The second innings followed the pattern of the first; the dog's amazing dexterity and speed over the ground and the quickness with which it returned the ball in its mouth to its master, left the result in no doubt.

A match on the Reading Recreation Ground in 1899 was played for a stake. Oscar Flint, landlord of the Victoria Arms in the town, backed himself and his dog Bingo to beat three players, Rogers, Thorp and Green. 'The scouting of the dog was of such a remarkable character that he enabled his owner to win by 17 runs to 15.'

George Brown of Sussex, whose lightning fast underarm deliveries had lethal effect, employed two long-stops. When playing for Brighton, one of the long-stops, 'Little' Dench, used to attach a sack of straw to his chest as protection: the other, on an occasion oft recounted, tried to stop a particularly fierce ball by hanging out his overcoat rather in the manner of a matador. Unfortunately, the ball brushed past the coat and killed a dog that had been prancing about behind.

Billy Buttress, one of the best spin bowlers of his day, was a gifted ventriloquist. He played for Cambridgeshire, Norfolk, Leicestershire, Devon, Cheshire and

Durham. Naturally this involved a lot of travelling and when in crowded railway carriages he practised to remarkable effect his imitation of a ferocious dog. Buttress was never short of a seat.

If Sunil Gavaskar, who suffers from cynophobia saw a dog on the field of play, he invariably lost his wicket.

Frederick Louis, Prince of Wales, eldest son of George II, was addicted – as were many of his aristocratic friends – to having a wager on cricket. He once organized a cricket match on horseback at Bromley with the Earl of Middlesex for a stake of £1,000, no mean sum in the 18th century. On the day, Middlesex's mounted batsmen were defeated by the Prince's equestrian bowlers. The umpires, of course, had to be doubly vigilant in anticipating appeals for lbw – any one of four legs could have been hit by the ball.

At a match at Tunbridge, Kent, in August, 1833, 'a gallant sergeant (one of the players) excited some amusement by mounting a horse and riding after the ball which had been struck with more than ordinary force'.

Walter Brearley, the Lancashire fast bowler, was not the greatest of batsmen. Invariably he batted at number eleven and his hurried gait to the wicket seemed to suggest that he himself did not wish to linger long. At any rate, when he appeared at Old Trafford, the horse that dragged the heavy roller used automatically to trot over to its place between the shafts as if it too recognized that the end of the innings was nigh.

In 1987, Richard Hadlee had a racehorse named after him. In the maiden race R H Horse managed seventh place, which is far short of the world-class New Zealand all-rounder's class.

A donkey caused a cup-tie to be replayed. The team from Lidget Green visiting Undercliffe for the match noticed that one end of the pitch was much damper than the other and protested vehemently. The groundsmen admitted that while pulling the roller the donkey had obeyed a call of nature. Undercliffe were banned from playing cup-ties at home for the remainder of the season unless the donkey could be persuaded to water both ends.

On 24 August, 1892, during a game in a field at Dover where some cattle were grazing, a bull suddenly bore down upon the players. They scattered desperately seeking cover, leaving the enraged beast to charge full tilt at the wickets, which he trampled out of the ground.

Bessie the cow caused a match to be abandoned before it had begun. The field where she chewed the cud adjoined the ground of Pentenstall Cricket Club in Bedfordshire. One summer's day Bessie decided she had had enough of the cud and so when a ball from a mighty six landed at her feet she seized the opportunity and chewed that instead. She also ate it. Unfortunately, it was the only one the club possessed.

At Goulburn, Australia, in December of 1876 James Lillywhite's English tourists took on

22 locals in a two-day match and won by 95 runs. On the first afternoon six hares and two kangaroos were seen on the ground while England were batting. A newspaper reported that the attendance of the kangaroos no doubt encouraged the fielders to 'pouch' a catch.

R B Van Wart, Scout Commissioner for Jodhpur, played a lot of cricket in India. He recalled many interruptions caused by unwanted visitors. Once two tigers trotted on to a pitch during a game, although admittedly they were only cubs belonging to the local Maharaja. At other times monkeys, wild pigs, bees and even innocuous butterflies caused suspensions of activity. And vicious kraits (a species of snake best left alone) hiding under the matting were wont to disturb the concentration of any batsman.

In June, 1895, the *Athletic News* reported five weasels running on to the pitch during a game at Darlington. They were chased away by a bat-waving player from the visiting Liverpool team and finally escaped down a hole on the bank of the River Skerne.

At Loretto School in July 1885, a rat emerged from its hole by the boundary at the wrong moment. The rodent stopped a hefty drive along the ground and was killed on the spot.

BOWLED OVER BIRDS

The most famous bird that had its feathers ruffled was a sparrow killed at Lord's by a ball bowled by Jehangir Khan (Cambs. University) to T N Pearce (MCC) on 3 July 1936.

The sparrow was mounted on the ball with which it was dispatched and is to be seen in a display-case in the Lord's Museum.

Bernhard Bentinck, attacking batsman for Hampshire Hogs and also Alton in August 1921, was dismissed by a ball which was deflected on to the wicket after striking and killing a swallow.

L O'B Fleetwood-Smith, talented spinner of unplayable corkscrew deliveries, used to sing popular songs and imitate bird calls while fielding. His speciality was the call of the magpie. Fleetwood-Smith ended his days on a vagrancy charge living the life of a derelict with the 'meths' drinkers on Melbourne's skid row.

A dead mackerel dropped from the beak of a seagull flying overhead caused some hilarity when it landed on the pitch during a game between Stowe Templars and Old Cliftonians at Bristol.

INSECT INCIDENCE

'A wicket-keeper, James Edwards, caught a wasp in mistake for the ball and was badly stung in a match on Hungerford Down in 1835.'

In 1890, Members of Parliament and the Press played a match on the Adelaide Oval. Midway through the afternoon the ground was covered with locusts which impeded the players and obliterated sight of the spectators in the pavilion when the insects rose in clouds.

If the South African tour to England in 1970 had taken place, a plan had been hatched by protesters whereby half-a-million locusts would be released onto cricket pitches, on which they were due to play, to eat the grass.

SHORT SHARK SHOCK

During a game on a matting wicket by the sea-shore at Sohar a ball was lofted towards the ocean and swallowed by a shark.
Authentication for this fishy story is to be found in the scorebook: c Fish b Birkat Ullah.

Kevin Sampson interrupted a game of beach cricket at Rivertown in New Zealand's South Island to kill a shark with his bat. The six-foot long 'Jaws' was threatening Sampson's nine-year-old son, Tony, who was offshore on his surfboard.

'I raced into the sea and banged the shark on the head with the bat,' said the aquatic cricketer, 'then I pulled it onto the beach by its tail and gave it a few more bangs. I don't know if I knew what I was doing until I had done it.' Play was quickly resumed.

(Daily Express)

101

CRICKET AND THE CHURCH

'Cricket is an idea, it is an idea of the Gods,' said J M Barrie, and it is quite likely that two monks, Eustathius Cartonius and Josephus Iscanus, early observers of basic bat and ball games, would have held the same view. Cricket and the Church have had a continuous and occasionally thorny relationship ever since the day when one heard about the other.

At Boxgrove in Sussex in 1622 some irreligious cricketers faced earthly retribution in the Court:

'I present Raphe West, Edward Hartley, Richard Slaughter, William Martin, Richard Martin junior, together with others in their company whose names I have no notice of for playing at cricket in the churchyard on Sunday the fifte of May after sufficient warning to the contrary, for three speciall reasons; first for that it is contrary to the 7th article; secondly for that they use to breake the church windows with the ball; and thirdly for that a little childe had like to have her braines beaten out with a cricket batt. And I also present Richard Martin senior and Thomas West the old churchwardens for defending and mayntayning them in it. Wee present Anthony Ward, servant to Mr Earle our Minister and Edward Hartley for playing cricket at evening prayer tyme on Sunday the xxviiith of April.'

In 1712, there were two publications that underlined the perils of not observing the Lord's Day. A broadside produced in Paternoster Row was entitled *The Devil and the Peers or, The Princely Way of Sabbath-Breaking. Being a true account of a famous Cricket Match between two Lords and two Boys on Sunday the 25th of May last . . . near Fern-Hill in Windsor Forrest: for Twenty Guineas.*

The other was a book of sermons called *The Sabbath-breakers, or a young man's dreadful warning-piece.* One of the exhortations was a record of what befell four youths who dared to play cricket near Maidenhead thicket on Sunday, 6 July. 'As they were at play, there rose out of the ground a Man in Black with a Cloven-foot which put them in a great Consternation; but as they stood in this frightened Condition, the Devil flew up in the Air, in a Dark Cloud with flashes of Fire, and in his room he left a very Beautiful Woman, and Robert Yates and Richard Moore hastily stepping up to her being Charm'd with her Beauty went to kiss her, but in the Attempt they instantly fell down Dead . . .'

The other two fellows who had not been quite so bold took to their beds and had not been seen since. Perhaps they had a hangover.

In 1747, the Rev. Henry Venn took his leave of cricket in true thespian mode. Having played for Surrey against England he threw down his bat, saying, 'Whoever wants a bat which has done me good service may take that, as I have no further occasion for it.' His fellow players enquiring of the reason were told, 'Because I am to be ordained on

Sunday and I will never have it said of me, "Well struck, Parson!"'

Clergymen, some of whom have been excellent players, have contrived, by appearing under assumed names, to play cricket without risking the wrath of their bishop. For instance, the Rev J Dolphin played as J Copford and took part in a match in 1831 that had a stake of £1,000 a side. Dolphin was known to donate a percentage of his winnings to worthy causes.

Lord Frederick Beauclerk, 'the finest player of his day' in the first part of the 19th century, was Vicar of St Albans, Hertfordshire for many years, though he 'ne'er preached once of a twelvemonth'. The noble Lord had a choleric nature and used to express himself forcibly. 'Wouldn't it be a good thing to have a change?' asked one of his team when Beauclerk had been bowling

a long time with little effect. 'Yes, it would,' replied the beaver-hatted Beauclerk, 'I'll change ends.'

As a youth, Cardinal Manning played cricket for Harrow and then when he had moved on to Oxford was a pupil of Charles Wordsworth, who one afternoon sent him a bat accompanied by a poetic epistle. Manning responded in kind, and one of his stanzas reads:

'The bat that you were kind enough to send,
Seems (for as yet I have not tried it) good;
And if there's anything on earth can mend
My wretched play, it is that piece of wood.'

Canon, the Rev F R Evans, nephew of the authoress George Eliot, appeared for two public schools, Cheltenham and Rugby, Oxford University (1863–5) and two counties, Warwickshire and Worcestershire. As a round-arm bowler he was no-balled in 1863 for delivering the ball with his arm too high. Evans spent 38 years as Rural Dean of Monks Kirby.

C T Studd, the most talented cricketer in a family of talented cricketers (he played for Eton, Cambridge, Middlesex and England), became a missionary in China and then later in India and the Belgian Congo. When in the Congo he helped build a church and made sure that the aisle was exactly 22 yards.

Dr Parr, smoking his pipe and supping from his jug, used to sit on the green at Halton in Warwickshire on Sunday

afternoons, and watch his parish lads play cricket. He would not allow those who did not go to church to take part.

A Hampshire clergyman in 1893 announced from the pulpit 'On Saturday we play the return cricket match with Tisted. I shall umpire on that occasion, when I trust that our united endeavours will meet with success.'

The Rev Disturnall, rector of Wormshill in Kent, was about to deliver his sermon when he suddenly caught sight of two bats and six stumps in a corner of the church. 'Before I begin,' he said, 'I wish to know whose bats are those which have been brought in the church?' 'Please, Parson, they be Bill Burgis's,' answered a young yokel. 'Bill Burgis's! Oh, well, let them be, for he's too lazy to break the Sabbath with them.'

Before a Roses match, Eddie Wainwright, Yorkshire all-rounder, used to kneel and pray in the dressing-room: 'Oh, God, if you're on our side, then we'll win. If you're on their side, then they'll win. But please, please God, just stay out of the way for the next three days so as we can thrash 'em.'

In March 1903, at Christ Church, Crowborough, Sussex the Rev G Hugh Jones preached a sermon entitled 'LBW: a parable of the Cricket Field'. He took his text from St Matthew xiii, 84.

Prebendary Wilson Carlile sermonized on 'Cricket

and Christianity' at St Mary-at-Hill, The Monument, London, 2 September 1906. Other discourses from Carlile centred on 'Surrey's New Bowler', 'C B Fry' and 'Warner or MacLaren?'. At this distance it is not known who was the Saviour and who was the sinner.

Canon F B R Browne, right-hand fast medium bowler for Sussex in the 1920s, had a somewhat eccentric delivery, all topsy-turvyish off the wrong foot. He was nicknamed 'Tishy' after a racehorse of the time who used to gallop in a rather strange manner.

In 1926, the Rev J F Denning of Hungerford, aged 72, took 214 wickets in local matches. In 1927, he dismissed four batsmen in four balls. The opposing skipper accused Denning of receiving divine guidance. The Reverend's response was a non-committal, beatific smile.

The Rev Canon J H Parsons had a most unusual career. He first played for Warwickshire prior to the First World War as a professional; post-war he appeared as a commissioned Army Captain, then again as a professional. In 1929 he was ordained and from then on he turned out as an amateur. A potential England player and a superb driver of fast bowling, in his time Parsons joined the select band of those who have played for both Gentlemen and Players. In his last match for Warwickshire in 1934, he made 94 out of 121 in two hours, including a dozen fours and three sixes. This 'captain's innings' saw them home by one wicket. He died in 1981, aged 90.

An Archdeacon took a holiday one Sunday, entrusting his parish to a colleague. When he returned his replacement reported, 'Capital congregation, and very well behaved, but I am very sorry to tell you that after church they all went off to cricket.' 'Of course they did,' was the reply, 'and if I had been here I should have gone with them.'

A Wiltshire clergyman was so enamoured of cricket that he suggested the church vestry be used as a pavilion and the hymn-board as a score-board.

A miner who had been on unamicable terms with his parson for many years one day met with an accident and asked him to visit. The visits continued and a friendship grew. 'What dispelled the antipathy?' asked the parson. 'Oh,' said the miner, 'that hit o' yourn to square-leg for six a fortnight ago converted me.'

One day Canon Lancelot Smith found himself in a predicament. During a game at Spalding in Lincolnshire he was not out as the lunch interval arrived. There was no time for refreshment as Smith was at that moment supposed to be conducting a funeral service. The resourceful Reverend hurriedly changed his gear, ran round to the church, made some judicious cuts in the order of service – feeling sure that his dead parishioner, a cricket lover, would understand – directed a successful internment and then returned in time to change back into his whites and walk out to the wicket with his partner as play resumed.

The Vicar of Much Slaughter in the Cotswolds sometimes played for the village side on Sunday afternoons. Fortunately, the ground was close to the church, as on one occasion he was late for his own evening service. He had been batting rather well, and only realized the time when an impatient member of the congregation rang the church bell to summon him from the crease. The Vicar made a spectacular exit then entrance by hurdling a boundary fence, sprinting up the church path and dashing into the pulpit hastily donning cassock and collar over his cricketing 'whites'. 'Let us play,' he gasped.

A recent newspaper report underlined the possibility of passover services at Lord's. The Liberal Jewish Synagogue near the ground had to undergo structural alterations and it was suggested that a marquee should be erected on the sacred turf. In years past, there was a close relationship between the first rabbi, Israel Mattuck and 'Plum' Warner, and when the synagogue had been bombed during the war services had been held in the pavilion.

The father-in-law of Lord Hume, C A Alington, Dean of Durham, well-known writer of detective stories and sometime Headmaster of Eton and Shrewsbury, where he employed Neville Cardus as a cricket professional, always maintained that St Cuthbert and the Venerable Bede would have made a wonderful pair of opening batsmen. He is quoted to have said, 'that he never walked down the nave of the Cathedral without wondering whether or not it took spin'.

Quipped cricketing cleric, Geoffrey Beck on taking 4 wickets in 4 balls for the National Book League against a team of authors: 'They were meant to be off-spinners when they left me. I don't know what they were when they arrived at the other end.'

As a lay preacher of a congregational chapel in Wales, Brian Rogers refused to play in Sunday matches for Gowerton CC. He therefore *watched* his side being narrowly defeated in the final of the Haig National Village Championship at Lord's.

The Rev David Sheppard (now Bishop of Liverpool) had managed to get very little practice before the England tour to Australia in 1962–63. He dropped a number of chances at slip. Fred Trueman, never short of advice, could not restrain his feelings when yet another snick went to ground: 'You might keep yer eyes shut when yer prayin', Vicar, but I wish you'd keep 'em open when I'm bowling!'

Stephen Green, curator of the MCC, sent a letter to *The Times* in June 1983:

'Sir, I do not know whether Cardinal Hume's election to membership of the MCC has any bearing on the matter, but I have just had a letter from Trinidad. It was addressed to *Lourdes* Cricket Ground.'

WOMEN AND CRICKET

'I doubt if there be any scene in the world more animating or delightful than a cricket match,' wrote Mary Mitford. The authoress was a spectator but there have been some notable female exponents throughout the years, not least Marjorie Pollard, Betty Snowball, Molly Hide, Rachael Heyhoe Flint, Mary Duggan, Janette Brittin and latterly Sarah Potter. 'Women's cricket should not be compared to

men's. They have their own style and skill which can be admired as such,' said Nancy Joy in her book, *Maiden Over*.

In 1745, in the very week in which the Young Pretender landed in Scotland, the first recorded women's match took place:

'The greatest cricket-match that

ever was played in the South part of England was on Friday, the 26th of last month (July) on Gosden Common, near Guildford, in Surrey, between eleven maids of Bramley and eleven maids of Hambleton, dressed all in white. The Bramley maids had blue ribbons and the Hambleton maids red ribbons on their heads. The Bramley girls got 119 notches and the Hambleton girls 127. There was of bothe sexes the greatest number that ever was seen on such an occasion. The girls bowled, batted, ran and catched as well as most men could do in that game.'

(*Reading Mercury*)

In 1765, 'A few days since, a cricket match was played at Upham, Hants, by eleven married against eleven maiden women, for a large plum cake, a barrel of ale and regale of tea, which was won by the latter. After the diversion the company met and drank tea: they spent the evening together and concluded it with a ball.'

The Duke of Hamilton was so smitten by Miss Elizabeth Burrell's leg, glanced during a 'ladies of quality' cricket encounter promoted by the Countess of Derby at the Oaks in 1777, that he married her without delay.

In July 1785 an article was penned in letter form to the editor of *The Rambler's Magazine*, describing an incident at a recent match at White Conduit Fields that was bizarre in the extreme. Under the title, 'The Cricket Ball Lost in a Furze Bush', the writer, pseudonymed 'a lover of the wicket', recounts how 'one of the balls was sent with such force and fury, that a lady who thought herself perfectly secured by distance from the scene of action, received it in a very improper place. As if enamoured of the lady's charms, it flew with such eagerness as to make her lose the centre of gravity and fall upon her back. For some time the ball was not to be found, on which the usual cry of 'a lost ball' was vociferd [sic] – but at length it came to light, and was taken from between the lady's legs, though not till after the adverse party had lost a notch by the delay . . .'

Extraordinary Female Cricket Match
'In a field belonging to Mr Story, at the back of Newington Green, near Ball's Pond, Middlesex, on Wednesday, 2 October, 1811, this singular performance, between the Hampshire and the Surrey Heroines (twenty-two females) commenced at eleven o'clock in the morning. It was made by two noblemen, for 500 guineas aside. The performers in this contest were of all ages and sizes, from fourteen to sixty, the young had by the colour of true blue, which were pinned in their bonnets, in the shape of the Prince's plume. The Surrey were equally as smart – their colours were blue, surmounted with orange. The latter eleven consisted of Ann Baker (sixty years of age, the best runner and bowler on that side), Ann Taylor, Maria Batfutt, Hannah Higgs, Elizabeth Gale, Hannah Collas, Hannah Bartlett, Maria Cooke, Charlotte Cooke, Elizabeth Stocke, and Mary Fry. The Hampshire eleven were Sarah Luff, Charlotte Pulain, Hannah Parker, Elizabeth Smith, Martha Smith, Mary Woodrow, Nancy Porter, Ann Poulters, Mary Nowell, Mary Hislock.' A name was missing.

Martha Grace, matriarch of W G, his four brothers and three sisters, constructively criticized their form at cricket. She once chided W G who had been caught off an indeterminate stroke: 'Willie, Willie, haven't I told you over and over again how to play that ball?'

Christina Willes used to bowl at her brother John in the barn of his home at Tonford near Canterbury. To avoid entanglement with her voluminous skirts she bowled round-arm. Willes adopted the style himself and tried to get it recognized. After he had been no-balled for bowling in this fashion at Lord's he rode away in a huff and never played again. His sister's invention became law a few years later. Precedence has also been claimed for another woman, Mrs Lambert, who bowled thus to her husband.

The first women's cricket club was founded at Nun Appleton, Yorkshire

in 1887 by eight ladies of aristocratic birth who were either close related or intimate friends. The *White Heather Cricket Club* initially consisted of The Hon M Brassey, The Hon B Brassey, Lady Milner, Lady Idina Nevill, Lady Henry Nevill, The Hon M Lawrence, Miss Chandos-Pole and Miss Street, but by 1891 had increased its membership to 50. They played against girls' schools, boys' preparatory schools and ladies' XIs. Lucy Ridsdale was perhaps the most celebrated member; she became wife of the Prime Minister, Stanley Baldwin. The Club flourished for many years and did not finally disband until the 1950s:

'The friendships we've formed in
    White Heather
May they grow and lengthen each
    link,
With a cheer 'Here's cricket for ever'
Neath the folds of white, green and
    pink.'

The Original English Lady Cricketers were formed in 1890. Two teams toured the country, used false names and were heavily chaperoned. The strain was too much. They disbanded after two seasons. Rockley Wilson saw them play at Llandudno. He said: 'They might be Original and English but they were neither Ladies nor Cricketers.' He was 10 at the time.

A hundred years ago, some ladies of the theatrical profession playing under assumed names pitted themselves against their male counterparts in a game at the Recreation Ground, Paddington. The gentlemen were handicapped by having to bat left-handed with broomsticks. They also had to field only with their left hand, the penalty for not doing so being a three-run addition to their

opponents' score. The ladies won by 37 runs.

The scorebook of a match between Ladies and Gentlemen at Ootacamund carries the entry for 1901: 'Lady E Lygon, retired weary, 60'. A conveyance was provided to carry the ladies back to their tent when dismissed.

Mabel Bryant scored 224 not out in 2¼ hrs for the Visitors against the Residents at Eastbourne, Sussex in August, 1901.

Rubina Humphries, aged 15, took all 10 wickets without conceding a run for Dalton Ladies v Woodfield Sports Club in June 1931. The feat was equalled by Rosemary White for Wallington Ladies v Beaconsfield Ladies in July, 1962.

In a match between two women's XIs in Melbourne in 1932, a complaint was lodged that 'one of the team had used chewing-gum to fix the bails to the wicket, so that the slow bowler, the bowler of lobs or sneaks had little chance of getting a wicket, even if she hit the stumps'.

Iris Clarke, a lady of indeterminate age but determined manner once stopped a Hampshire 2nd XI game. A hit from Robin Smith had smashed a ball right through the window of her flat overlooking the county ground at Southampton. Mrs Clarke was not amused. She stalked onto the pitch and left the players in no doubt about her feelings towards those who played silly games that damaged people's property and endangered the lives of old ladies sitting at home minding their own business when all of a sudden etc. etc. etc. After she had harangued all about her for five minutes and with both players and spectators getting extremely restless as Mrs Clarke still refused to return the ball and leave the field, the promise of remuneration won the day. The lady huffily retired whence she came, muttering imprecations.

In the vicinity of Christchurch, New Zealand, there was a small and delightfully picturesque cricket ground that was known as 'The Valley of Peace'. Many felt the name was a natural reflection of the surroundings but, in fact, it was given because women were not allowed to set foot on unadulterated masculine turf.

J C Clay, Glamorgan's skilful off-spinner, who played several matches for Wales between 1923–6, one Test for England in 1935 and eventually became a post-war Test selector, was a skilful humorous essayist. Part of one of Clay's articles deserves to be reproduced here:

Birth Control
'Of recent years women have been taking to cricket more and more, and the following suggestions, which I flatter myself are eminently practical, while being also romantic, show how the problem of England's cricketing future should be tackled.

The MCC (stand up, please, as a mark of respect) should appoint a select committee to draw up a list of all the best men and women cricketers and should endeavour to arrange suitable alliances between them. This is putting it very much in a nutshell, as I quite realize that

it will be a tricky business and require much knowledge and tact. It may be wrong, for instance, to assume that the union of a male fast and a female googly bowler will produce an unplayable type embodying the pace of one and the finger spin of the other. Breeders of high-class bloodstock will tell you that the mating of two extremes, a stayer and a sprinter, seldom achieves the happy medium, which, theoretically, it should do. It will, therefore, be necessary to co-opt, I think, one or two members of the Jockey Club on the Committee.

Of course, this is all going to cost money, and I would suggest that the MCC (pause for silent prayer) set aside a special fund for the purpose. Those who, with the committee's approval, propose getting married would receive a small grant on signing bills of lading or whatever the term is, and a substantial sum on each male child produced. It is obvious that most money must be given on the COD basis, because you can't trust some of these young men nowadays. Very briefly, such is my proposal for the betterment of English cricket. It will take time and labour, but the results will surely justify themselves.

I forgot to add that the fees of the members of the committee should be about £500 per year each. I am prepared to serve on it.'

In his book *Playing Days*, former England captain Tony Lewis recalls one of his most embarrassing moments: 'I left the 1962 University match and travelled to join the Glamorgan team at Bath for a match against Somerset. I had a £500 overdraft in the bank but my fiancée, Joan, who had gone home to Neath, teaching to save for a year, had collected £350 in the bottom drawer! By the end of this same Somerset match, the savings and the fiancée had gone.

'It was hot, sunny weather. Glamorgan were in the field. My captain, Ossie Wheatley, sent me to third man with the instruction, "Take a look at that while you are down on the boundary, A.R." He pointed to a young lady, dressed attractively under a black, wide-brimmed straw hat which shielded her face. Nice shape, I thought, good legs. I had got within 20 yards when the brim of the hat lifted suddenly, like a visor. It was Joan. "Hi," I said. "Thought you were at home. Great to see you." I should have detected by the firm-footed stance and the folded arms that she was at battle stations.

'She marched a dozen yards infield, over the boundary line; embarrassing in front of hundreds of Somerset spectators perched on temporary stands in that quarter of the ground. She then made her speech. "If it is your wish to take the Bishop of Portsmouth's daughter to the Christ's Marguerites' cocktail party and not me, then you can jolly well marry her." Next, in a ceremony cheered loudly by the Somerset fans, she removed her engagement ring from the third finger, drew back her arm like a javelin thrower, and hurled it at me. Spectators were now on their feet clapping as she turned on her high-heels and left.

'First-class cricket is best played with a clear mind and I cannot say that I concentrated on a single ball bowled from then on. There is something distinctly uncomfortable about fielding with your engagement ring back in your pocket.

'I saw her drive away in a gleaming new Mini – she had blown her savings.

'We were married three weeks later.'

In 1981 at Canterbury, Bob Woolmer of Kent hit a cracking six into the crowd. 'Amid the warning shouts and ducking of heads, a white-haired lady calmly and cleanly caught the ball and tossed it coolly to the nearest fielder, who graciously invited her to join in the game. England could do with her.'

113

The highest recorded score made by a woman is Jan Molyneaux's 298 for Olympic v Northcote, Melbourne Grade 'A' Final, 1967.

Mrs Shirley Morgan showed that women can hold the whip-hand even at cricket. In 1983 at Mountain Ash in Wales, she arrived at the local ground to help with the teas. One of the side failed to turn up so Mrs Morgan was hastily co-opted, opened the innings, top-scored with 51, took 2 wickets for 21 in six overs and held a catch. It goes without saying that her team emerged victorious.

A local lad was sent by his wife to get some salt to accompany the almost-ready Sunday lunch. Passing the cricket green where the village side were just about to start a match, he was cajoled into making up the numbers. Forgetting entirely that he was on an errand, he took the field with the rest of the side and play

commenced. About an hour later his irate wife stomped onto the pitch carrying his lunch on a tray. She then subjected him to verbal abuse and none too gently up-ended the meal over his head.

A Test match between England and India at Collingham, Leeds in 1986 ended as a draw with slow handclapping and tears. England were 25 runs short of victory. The Indians' slow over rate – 7 overs in the final hour – had provoked a stream of complaints. 'It was incredible,' said one spectator. 'They were sitting down on the pitch, complaining about crowd noise and demanding that cars be removed because of sunshine reflections from their windscreens. English players actually moved some of the cars and in the end there was a tannoy announcement asking us all to form a human wall in front of the others to try to get over the problem.' After a series of conflicting accusations and much friction, peace was finally restored.

LITERARY LINKS

The thread between the pen and the popping crease has been notably strong. Whether the characters were fictional cricketers, like Lord Peter Wimsey and Raffles or whether as was the case with E W Hornung's brother-in-law Conan Doyle, they were based on the names of actual players is, in a way, irrelevant. The deeds of one lot of practitioners inspired the prose of the other.

John Brand, a considerable player of the early 19th century, shut himself into a convent to compile an Armenian dictionary. He died in a lunatic asylum.

Charles Dickens' home at Gad's Hill was the scene of a number of charity matches and the novelist usually gave a guinea if the first ball – which he often bowled – was hit to the boundary.

Hans Christian Andersen played cricket at Gad's Hill in 1857.

Oscar Wilde disapproved of cricket because he said that 'the batting posture is positively indecent'.

Arthur Conan Doyle, no mean cricketer – he once took the wicket of W G Grace and played minor county and MCC games – is thought to have used or adapted the names of contemporary cricketers for his Sherlock Holmes stories. In 1972, the President of the United States Cricket Association, John I. Marder, drew up a list of over 400 characters with cricketing connections. The name of the great detective himself was believed to have come from a union of two Notts players, Mordecai *Sher*win and Frank Shack*lock* and Holmes from R S Hol*m*es, the cricket writer, or Henry Holmes of Hants. Brother Mycroft Holmes was obviously linked to William Mycroft of Derbyshire. As for the evil Professor Moriarty, Marder's conclusion was that 'no cricketer could stoop so low'.

Lewis Carroll, who took Alice to Wonderland, described an occasion when he was asked to bowl. 'I delivered,' he said, 'a simple ball which, I was told, had it gone far enough, would have been a wide.'

Joseph Wells, father of novelist H G Wells, was an all-rounder who played seven games for Kent in 1862-63. He took 4 wickets in 4 successive balls against Sussex.

J M Barrie formed his own side, the Allahakbarries. The peculiar name was coined from the Arabic for 'Heaven help us' when the players were journeying in trepidation to their first match. Barrie himself was a slow enough left-arm bowler to run and stop the ball before it reached the batsman if he did not like the delivery.

P G Wodehouse's fictional butler and manservant 'Jeeves' was named after the Warwickshire fast bowler, Percy Jeeves, who was killed in action at Montaubon, France in 1916.

The hilarious happenings of poet J C Squire's (later Sir John Squire) team, The Invalids, were reflected in A G MacDonell's *England, Their England*. Members of the side included G K Chesterton, Hilaire Belloc, Alec Waugh and J B Priestley.

The poet, Siegfried Sassoon, captained his own team the *Siegfried Sassoon Estate Eleven* in several encounters. He once exchanged copies of Nyren's *Young Cricketers Tutor* with yet another poet, Edmund Blunden and inserted a skit 'in the style of William Shakespeare' about the book, written in green ink. Blunden played several times in the Keats–Shelley Memorial Match at Hampstead.

'What do you think of the Test?' George Bernard Shaw was once asked. The 'Old Man' affected puzzlement. 'What are they testing?' he queried.

In Geoffrey Whitelock's monograph *Cricket in the Writings of James Joyce* there are many references to the game to be found. One example is in Joyce's 'markedly autobiographical novel' *A Portrait of the Artist as a Young Man*. The hero, Stephen Dedalus attends Clongowes Wood College:

'But there was no play on the football grounds for cricket was coming and some said that Barnes (*William Barnes, the Notts medium-pacer was coach at Clongowes in the year, 1888, that Joyce joined the College*) would be prof. and some said it would be Flowers (*Wilfred Flowers, Notts all-rounder*). And all over the playgrounds they were playing rounders and bowling twisters and lobs. And from here and from there came the sounds of the cricket bats through the soft grey air. They said: Pick, pack, pock, puck: little drops of water in a fountain slowly falling in the brimming bowl.'

Joyce's younger brother, Stanislaus remarked that James disliked football but liked cricket and promised to be a useful bat. He 'eagerly studied the feats of Ranji and Fry, Trumper and Spofforth. I remember having to bowl for him for perhaps an hour at a time in our back garden in Richmond Street. I did so out of pure goodness of heart since, for my part, I loathed the silly, tedious, inconclusive game, and would not walk across the road to see a match.'

Samuel Beckett is, so far, the only Nobel Prize-winner for Literature to have appeared in *Wisden's Cricketers*

Almanack. He opened both the batting and bowling for Dublin University against Northants in 1926.

Karl Auty, an American cricket-lover from Chicago kept all his copies of *Wisden's Almanack* on specially constructed wooden runners underneath his bed – rather like eminent members of the judiciary are supposed to do with the stories of Billy Bunter in *The Magnet*. Auty eventually acquired a large collection of all types of cricket book which he bequeathed to Ridley College, St Catherine's, Ontario.

In 1974, during a game at the Sydney Cricket Ground, the British poet and author Laurie Lee was knocked unconscious by a flying beer bottle thrown from the notorious 'Hill'. Recovering later, Lee commented: 'I enjoyed it, but if I go back again I will wear a tin hat.'

Richard Gordon qualified as a doctor. He has said that he did not like his patients therefore he became an anaesthetist because they were asleep. Self-described as 'the world's worst cricketer' he played for *Punch* magazine in a match in which the captain made him field behind a tree – 'an enormous tree'.

THE ROAR OF THE GREASEPAINT, THE SMELL OF THE CROWD

A good proportion of those who practise Entertainment – on the concert platform, through the organs of press and broadcast, or in the theatre and on the screen – have always loved cricket. It provides a different sort of stage yet contains an essential ingredient – a huge audience, at least, for the prestigious games. So whether it's a dissolute 18th century 'rogue and vagabond', James Dance, who wrote an heroic poem about the game or John Nyren, of Hambledon fame, who entertained gipsies with his fiddle to save his father's poultry or even a latterday Peter Sellers, who photographed a descending ball when he should have been catching it, the love affair has remained constant.

MUSIC

John Small, a larger-than-life figure in Hambledon cricket not only made bats and balls but also violins and 'cellos. He twice used musical instruments to extricate himself from difficult situations. The story of his being trapped in a field with an angry bull and charming the animal into docility with a tune on his bass viol has been regaled many times. Not so well known was the occasion when Small was walking alongside a field in which a cricket match was being played. The batsman made a fierce hit and just as the ball was about to strike Small on the head he saved himself from injury in interposing his violin. It is possible both ball and fiddle bore Small's insignia although after inspecting the damage to sound-post and finger-board he might have

decided that he should have let himself be crowned instead. An epitaph for Small reads:

Here lies, bowl'd out by DEATH's
    unerring fall,
A CRICKETER renowned, by name
    JOHN SMALL;
But though his name was *small* yet
    great his fame,
For nobly did he play the 'noble
    game'.
His *life* was like his *innings* – long
    and good,
Full ninety summer he had DEATH
    withstood,
At length the ninetieth winter
    came – when (Fate
Not leaving him one solitary *mate*)
This last of *Hambledonians*, old JOHN
    SMALL,
Gave up his BAT and BALL – *his
    LEATHER, wax and all.*

One of the first, if not *the* first, cricket songs to survive is *Assist all ye muses, and join to rehearse, An Old English sport never praised yet in verse.* The song was adapted for the Hambledon Club in the 1770s by the Rev Reynell Cotton, author of *Universal Dictionary*, and Master of Hyde Abbey School, Winchester.

'Then fill up your glass, he's the best
    that drinks most.
Here's the Hambledon Club! – who
    refuses the toast?
Let's join in the praise of the bat and
    the wicket,
And sing in full chorus the patrons
    of cricket.'

The ditty may have started life in a production of David Garrick's at the Theatre Royal, Drury Lane in

1761, from whence it journeyed to Kent with new words to celebrate a Kentish victory over Hampshire. The Rev Cotton perhaps thought that the wrong side had been praised and set to work accordingly.

The first known visual link between cricket and music is to be found on the front cover of a piano piece entitled *The Village Rondo* by Matthias Holst. The picture depicts a rural scene with musicians and dancers in front of a tent, children playing cricket with two stump wickets in front of an inn, a school and church in the background and a

goat in the foreground. The Rondo was published between 1812 and 1815 and the composer is the great-grandfather of Gustav Holst, composer of *The Planets*.

Only one first-class fixture was ever played at the Sparth Bottoms Ground, Castleton Glebe, Rochdale. In June 1876 Lancashire beat Kent there by 10 wickets. On that occasion, the local brass band played at the same time as the cricketers. The musicians were seated next to the scoring tent and as the umpires preferred to call out rather than signal wides, no-balls, byes, etc., registering the correct total became rather a fraught operation. It was definitely a case of the Oom-pahs from the band being louder than the Um-pires in the middle.

The Hon Alfred Lyttelton, Eton, Cambridge, Middlesex, England and a barrister to boot, defended the French composer, Charles Gounod, in a libel action. In a recent issue of *Private Eye*, a reader likened Mike Gatting to another French composer, Claude Debussy. Worth a suit?

She is my cricketing girl, my love, my queen!
Each day, to watch the play, upon the field she is seen,
I'll make a match of my own with this sweet pearl,
I mean to make a long stop with my cricket girl.

The author of this vocal novelty, so described, was one Frank Leo and he wrote it for the music hall singer Sable Fern – her latest big hit! The sentiments of the song had, no doubt, been nurtured in real life as Leo and Fern conducted a rather indiscreet affair that led eventually to a scandal. The lady's husband learned of their assignations and in a fit of jealous rage made unsuccessful attempts to kill both of them before turning the gun on himself.

CRICKETERS WHO ALSO PLAYED . . .

W E Astill, the Leicestershire and England all-rounder who played during the first part of this century, was an accomplished singer who accompanied himself at the keyboard. He also played billiards and the ukelele, though not at the same time.

Colin Blythe, the Kent and England left-arm spinner, perhaps second only to Wilfred Rhodes in their day, played the violin. Blythe lost his life in World War I, depriving the game of one of its most subtle practitioners.

James Cutmore, who played for Essex between 1924 and 1936, reached 1,000 runs in 11 of those seasons. He possessed a fine tenor voice.

Surrey and England fast bowler, Maurice Allom, played tenor saxophone in a group called the Quinquaginta Club Ramblers, who were led by the well-known jazz pianist Fred Elizalde.

Frank Parr, Lancashire wicket-keeper in the '50s, played trombone in a traditional jazz group.

Mr Donald Bradman (as he was then) made a piano recording of *Old-fashioned Locket* and *Bungalow of Dreams* in the 1930s.

Cambridge contemporaries, Eddie Craig, Lancashire opening bat and two England captains, Tony Lewis of Glamorgan and Mike Brearley, Middlesex, all have musical accomplishments – Craig as a pianist, Brearley on clarinet and Lewis as a fine violinist and once leader of the National Youth Orchestra of Wales.

MUSICIANS WHO ALSO PLAYED . . .

The revered conductor, Sir Thomas Beecham, was captain of cricket at Rossall School.

Gerald Moore, who made the piano accompanist respectable, recalls in Michael Meyer's *Summer Days* how John Christie, founder of Glyndebourne Opera, reacted after a singing audition by Roy Henderson. Christie had attended the session together with musical director Fritz Busch and producer Carl Ebert. The two Germans were delighted with Henderson's singing but doubtful about his dramatic ability. 'Can he act?' they asked. 'Of course,' replied Christie, 'he's a cricketer.'

William Primrose, the respected viola player, often used to go for 'a net' at the Alf Gover indoor cricket school. He once faced-up to Herbert Strudwick, 'Struddy', the old Surrey and England wicket-keeper, who bowled him 3 times in an over of 6 balls. 'Struddy' was over 60 at the time and said that he had only bowled one over in his whole career in county cricket.

Julian Bream, the eminent guitarist, has been known to take the field wearing gloves in order to protect his fingers which, of course, are his livelihood, from possible damage.

Patrick Moore who, besides being an astronomer, has composed an opera and plays a very respectable xylophone, is perhaps not the most agile of cricketers. Nevertheless he once scored 50 – the *high*light of his sporting career.

Vic Lewis, artists' agent; professional musician, founder of the Vic Lewis Orchestra, organizer of the Show Business Cricket Team, representative of the United States Cricket Association, member of MCC and Middlesex and collector of *3,000 cricket ties*.

Martin Loveday, leader of the BBC Concert Orchestra, played for Surrey Colts.

Harrison Birtwhistle, reclusive and elemental British composer, was batting obdurately one day, only to be hit by the ball in a most tender spot. John Amis, music broadcaster, was fielding at silly point and recalls: 'I can see Harry's face going into a sort of smiling rictus, and he goes down very, very slowly on his knees. "Harry, is it your balls?" I ask him. Heavy breathing is the only reply. Julian Bream arrives from cover (without his gloves) and suggests rubbing them. "Don't rub 'em,' gasps Harry. "Count 'em!"'

Bramwell Tovey, conductor of the Sadlers Wells Royal Ballet and the newly reformed D'Oyly Carte, was given his unusual Christian name in honour of the founding family of the Salvation Army. Tovey in turn helped found a cricket team that was called 'Poets and Peasants' after the overture by Suppé.

CRICKETING SONGS

'Captain Sensible', aka Percy Pavilion, produced a disc called *The Cricket EP* in 1983, which was recorded at The Old Barn Studios in tropical Croydon. Side one includes a song entitled *Dolly Mixture* (dedicated to Basil d'Oliveira) and side two begins with *Mercenaries Cricket Club*, with the instruction please play loudly to J Carlisle, MP. The following year, the same company brought out *Gower Power*.

Colin Wilkie wrote and recorded a song in Germany in 1982 titled *Jim Laker took all Ten.*

That talented and versatile entertainer, Richard Stilgoe, who can play *When the Saints Go Marching In* on 18 different musical instruments (he says that is all he can play on any of them) has written over 20 cricket songs. Not many over, but enough. The one that is heard most often is called *Lilian Thomson*:

Ev'ry morning on the radio, the
   news comes to Australia
The English batsmen once again
   have had a ghastly failure
It was Lilian Thomson's bowling
   once again caused the collapse
I always thought Test Cricket was
   intended just for chaps
But Lilian Thomson is Australia's
   finest flower
A maiden bowling overs at a
   hundred miles an hour.

She's the fastest lady bowler that the
   world has ever seen
Her bumper's awe-inspiring and her
   language far from clean
Just imagine the reaction of Greig or
   Knott or Amiss
As this six foot six of Sheila runs up,
   do you wonder they miss?
She hit Randall on the ankle, then
   she hit him on the forehead
She finds the happy medium she
   could hurt him something horrid.
She's Lilian Thomson, the first of
   cricket's dames
A mixture of Joan Sutherland, Rolf
   Harris, or Clive James
She'll hit you on the temple, in the
   groin or knee and kidney,
To prove that liberated Adelaide's as
   good as Sydney.

Tim Rice, co-writer of *Chess* and many other musicals, much prefers cricket. He founded his own team 'The Heartaches' and produces an almanack, recording their glorious defeats that now seems set to rival the longevity of *Wisden*. With Andrew Lloyd Webber, he wrote a 25-minute show called *Cricket* which was put on for one performance at Windsor Castle in 1987. Her Majesty, The Queen was said to have been 'amused'.

MEDIA

For many years the urbane Chairman of the BBC Radio programme *Any Questions* was Freddie Grisewood. Grisewood often used to present programmes to do with cricket: in 1908 he played in one match for Worcestershire.

Francis Worsley, producer of one of radio variety's most famous programmes, *ITMA*, played cricket for Glamorgan during the club's Cinderella days in the 1920s. One of the sketches in *ITMA*'s run was

Letter to The Times:
*'Is there no way in which
Richards of Hampshire could be
co-opted into the English Test
side? Can no patriotic English
girl be persuaded to marry
him? He is quite personable
and surely such a sacrifice
would qualify him for selection.
Failing that, could not some
elderly gentleman adopt him?*

Yours faithfully,

Ned Sherrin
Producer, director, writer and performer'

dubbed 'Chinese Cricket'.
Apparently there was no
connection.

'Teddy' Wakelam, who gave the first
television Test match commentary –
England v Australia at Lord's,
1938 – was fond of relating a story of
the village cricketer who, when
asked how his team had fared,
replied: 'First we went in, then they
went in and we went in, and they
went in, and they won. Then they
went in and we went in, and they
went in, and we went in, and we
won. And then it were tea-time.'

Alistair Cooke, talking on the radio
about a Test match at Lord's, said:
'The general atmosphere of Lord's is
more like that of a prayer meeting
than a ball game . . . could be, of
course, everybody was simply
praying for the English team.'

THE STAGE

The comedian, James Love, whose
real name was Dance, penned some
verses in 1744 entitled *Cricket: an
heroic poem*, describing a match
played between Kent and England
at the Artillery Ground in June of
that year. The poem was reprinted
four times in the 18th century with
a further reproduction in 1922,
edited by F S Ashley-Cooper. Some
of it reads:

Hail CRICKET! glorious, manly,
    British Game!
First of all Sports! be first alike in
    Fame!
To my fir'd Soul thy busy Transports
    bring,
That I may feel they Raptures, while
    I sing;
And thou, kind Patron of the
    mirthful Fray,
SANDWICH, they Country's Friend,
    accept the Lay!
Tho' mean my Verse, my Subject yet
    approve,
And look propitious on the Game
    you love!

When the retiring Sun begins to
    smile,
And sheds its Glories round this sea-
    girt Isle;
When new-born Nature deck'd in
    vivid Green,
Chances dull Winter from the
    charming Scene:
High panting with Delight, the
    jovial Swain
Trips it exulting o'er the Flow'r-
    strew'd Plain;
They pleasures, CRICKET! all his
    Heart controul;
They eager Transports dwell upon
    his Soul:
He weighs the well-turn'd Bat's
    experienced'd Force,
And guides the rapid ball's
    impetuous Course,
His supple Limbs with nimble
    Labour plies,
Nor bends the Grass beneath him as
    he flies.
The joyous Conquests of the late
    flown Year,
In Fancy's Paint, with all their
    Charms appear,
And now again he views the long
    wish'd Season near,
O thou, sublime Inspirer of my
    Song!

What matchless Trophies to thy
  Worth belong!
Look round the Globe, inclin'd to
  Mirth, and see
What daring Sport can claim the
  Prize from thee!

William Yardley, drama critic and
writer of farces, had an eventful
start to his cricket career. As a boy at
Rugby he threw a cricket ball 100
yds with his right hand and 78 yds
with his left and as a young man at
Cambridge he scored the first ever
century in an inter-varsity match
against Oxford in 1870. Yardley
scored another century in the same
fixture two years later. His county
was Kent. The first Champion
County v The Rest match in 1901
was played for the benefit of his
widow.

Another drama critic Sir Max
Beerbohm, subscribed one shilling
to W G Grace's testimonial fund 'not
because he approved of cricket but
to show his detestation of golf'.

So far as is known, the only time
that county cricketers as a team
have ever played the game on the
West End stage was when the
famous theatrical impresario Sir
Oswald Stoll mounted a variety
spectacle for his winter season of
1908. The billing read *Surrey v
Middlesex*, four professionals from
the Oval captained by Alan Marshal
against like number from Lord's
who were led by Albert Trott and
included J T Hearne and the 19-year-
old 'Patsy' Hendren. The audience
were given a scorecard with the
programme so that those who
wished to could keep a check on the
official scorer who was kept busy
with chalk, duster and blackboard
on the stage itself.
    The painting on the backcloth
was of a village green surrounded
by trees on a perfect summer's day –

pastorally idyllic. The pitch was
restricted to 15 yards and local rules
applied; for instance, a hit meant a
run had to be attempted. The
umpires wore evening dress which
lent an air of authority. The runs
scored at each performance were
accumulative and each morning the
revised score was posted outside the
theatre – the game was being played
over a week – and by the Wednesday
Middlesex were leading by 11, 136
to Surrey's 125.
    At one performance, the net
which protected orchestra and
audience from the four-ounce ball
got stuck in some way, and the
game proceeded with those in the
stalls acting as auxiliary fielders.
Miraculously, no one was injured.
The stunt continued neck-and-neck
for the remainder of the week and
at the final performance Middlesex
just managed to win the cup.

A notice announced the appearance
of F C Holland at a London Music
Hall described him as the
'Celebrated *Saucy* Cricketer'. The
notice should, of curse, have read
'Celebrated *Surrey* Cricketer'.

Basil Foster, middle-order batsman
who played for Malvern,
Worcestershire and Middlesex was
an actor on the London stage. Foster
was one of the 'Fostershire'
brotherhood, seven in all, who
played for Worcestershire; there
were also two nephews, C K who
also adopted the Worcestershire
colours and P G who played for
Kent. Basil Foster had a cricketing
understudy in a production of *The
Dollar Princess* at Daly's Theatre –
N A Knox, Dulwich, Surrey and
England fast bowler.

Oscar Asche, whose real name was
John Stanger Heiss, English actor

and lyricist of Scandinavian descent, born in Australia, remembered chiefly for his smash-hit oriental musical fantasy *Chu Chin Chow*, played cricket at minor county level. He liked to describe himself as 'a rotund striker' and on the night of one Eton and Harrow match he wanted all the robbers in *Chu Chin Chow* to carry miniature cricket bats on to the stage. Asche was with Sir Frank Benson's company for some years; they shared a love of cricket and a detestation of *slow* cricket. His invective was once turned against J W Hearne at Lord's – Hearne had been labouring somewhat – 'How I would like that fellow to play Desdemona to my Othello, because I should enjoy strangling the life out of his carcass.'

Cyril Ritchard reflected the uproar caused by the 'Bodyline' tour of Australia in 1932/33 when he added an extra verse to a song in *Our Miss Gibbs*, in which he was appearing in His Majesty's Theatre, Sydney:

Now this new kind of cricket takes
*   courage to stick it,*
There's bruises and fractures galore,
After kissing their wives and insuring
*   their lives*
Batsmen fearfully walk out to score.
With a prayer and a curse, they prepare
*   for the hearse*
Undertakers look on with broad grins,
Oh, they'd be a lot calmer in Ned Kelly's
*   armour*
When Larwood the wrecker begins.

Donald Sinden in *Laughter in the Second Act* recalls 'A War of the Roses cricket match (that) was played (at Stratford) in which Peggy Ashcroft led the Lancastrians and I the Yorkists. Her team had Cyril Washbrook as honorary captain and mine had Len Hutton. You need to know your history to appreciate why Brewster Mason as the Earl of

Warwick was the umpire. Politically the result of the match had to be a draw.'

John Le Mesurier, the character actor who starred in *Dad's Army* and who died in 1983, was a purposeful right-hand batsman who played for the Gentlemen of Suffolk many times during the 1930s.

Peter Gibbs, Oxford University, Staffordshire and Derbyshire opening batsman, has written several critically acclaimed radio plays.

Eric Sykes, comic actor, was not laughing on the occasion he kept wicket to Fiery Fred Trueman at a charity match. He foolhardily stopped a lethal delivery that pushed his finger out at a tangent. 'Look at that,' demanded the injured Sykes to Trueman. 'What's wrong with it?' replied Fred. 'It's bent,' yelled Sykes. 'All actors are bent,' was the quick rejoinder.

The playwright Tom Stoppard helped raise money for all-weather pitches at Merchant Taylors School in 1983 by signing a special limited edition of 500 copies of a cricketing extract from his play *The Real Thing*.

Jimmy Tarbuck, on a television tribute to Dickie Henderson, shortly after the West Indies tour in 1986:
   'Why is everybody getting at the England cricket team? After all, they've done nothing. I rang them up the other day to wish them luck and was told they'd just gone in to bat. I said, "That's all right, I'll wait".'

Sir Frank Benson, actor-manager, best remembered for his touring Shakespearian company, maintained a balanced view between cricket and the stage. On sending for a replacement he wired: 'Wanted, a slow left-arm bowler to play Cassius'.

Trevor Howard, who is remembered affectionately as a forceful screen actor rather than stage performer, insisted that any work contract should contain a clause allowing time off for Test matches. He even had a matinée changed to another day in order that he could watch cricket. Inevitably, however, an offer arrived that he could not refuse – a film in Jamaica with Cary Grant. At breakfast on the first morning at the location hotel, Howard was thinking wistfully of the Test match that was starting that day at Lord's. Suddenly, the waiter came up to his table which he was sharing with the director and producer. 'It's raining, sir,' he said. The two movie bosses looked alarmed then immediately dashed outside to see for themselves – raining in Jamaica, at this time of year, with over 1,000 extras lined up on the beach waiting for shooting to begin. The cost did not bear contemplation – dollars would be disappearing as fast as water down a drain. The waiter, who shared the actor's affinity with cricket, had returned to the kitchen and once

more came to the table with the news: 'There's no play before lunch. I heard it on the radio.'

There have been a number of theatrical teams – notably the Thespids, the Stage XI and, more recently, the Lord's Taverners. The side, however, that acquired a special place in public imagination was the **Hollywood Cricket Club.**

In the 1930s, the Hollywood Cricket Club was synonymous with the name of C Aubrey Smith; England and Sussex, West End and Broadway, Hollywood's archetypal English gentleman actor in over a hundred films. Although Smith did not actually found the Club, his celebrated status in the environs of movieland enabled him to 'persuade' stars to turn out at matches and give the Club a prominence in their early years. Some stars came to play, others just came.

Among the first Club members directly or indirectly connected with the film industry were Claude King, Alan Mowbray, Stanley Mann, Herbert Marshall, Philip Merivale, Reginald Owen, Pat Somerset and then, a little later, Melville Cooper, Fausto Acke, Douglas Walton, Frank Lawton, Nigel 'Willie' Bruce and H B Warner.

At the inaugural meeting of the cricket club, P G Wodehouse took the minutes and offered to help buy some of the equipment. Wodehouse, of course, in his schooldays had been a capable cricketer for Dulwich College: he was made a vice-president of Hollywood CC together with Ronald Colman, Leon Errol and George Arliss.

Racial snobbery reared 'horrorifically' when somebody objected to the membership of Boris Karloff, the son of a diplomat in the Indian Civil Service. Fortunately the objection was overruled immediately.

On his first arrival in California when staying at the Château Marmont, a one-time haven for all British actors when working in LA, it is reported that Laurence Olivier found a note from Aubrey Smith which read: 'There will be net practice tomorrow at 4 pm. I trust I shall see you there.' Olivier turned out once at least, and borrowed Karloff's cricket boots.

David Niven played more frequently and he was no mean performer on the field. In a game against Pasadena he batted at number 5 in a side that included three England captains, two former, one current. 'Gubby' Allen top scored with 77, C B Fry hit 12, Aubrey Smith did not bat and David Niven managed 13.

In 1939 another one-time England captain visited Hollywood – 'Archie' MacLaren, who had first played against Aubrey Smith, also in Hollywood, when making his debut for Lancashire in 1890. MacLaren enjoyed a couple of days filming as a Crimean War veteran in *The Four Feathers*. Smith took the part of General Burroughs in the film and he had secured the 'extra work' for MacLaren in order that between 'takes' 'we would have a good chance to have a decent natter'.

An oft quoted Aubrey Smith tale occurred in 1932, when an Australian side organized by Arthur Mailey were finishing a tour of Canada and the USA with some matches in Los Angeles. The events are authenticated by none other than Sir Donald Bradman who was one of the party.

In one of the games Smith was fielding at slip and dropped a catch, which was a noteably rare event even in his 70th year. 'The Don', who was at the non-striker's end, remembers him holding up the game and with an imperious wave of his arm calling out to Fred Loehndorf, who was his German chauffeur and 'man about the house', to bring him his spectacles.

This was dutifully done – C Aubrey put them on and signalled to the umpire that the game should resume. The bowler sent down a good length delivery, which provoked a further snick from the edge of the bat and the ball flew towards slip where Smith fumbled and dropped another catch. There was a stunned silence and an interminable pause at the unheard-of happenings. Two catches dropped off two balls. Smith took off his spectacles and inspected them at arm's length. A loud expostulation was immediately forthcoming: 'Egad,' he cried, 'the clown's brought me my reading glasses!'

General Burroughs: Do you remember Wilmington?
General Faversham: Wilmington?

Burroughs: Fine old service family. Father killed at Inkermann, grandfather blown up under Nelson, an uncle scalped by Indians – oh, splendid record, splendid.
Faversham: What happened?
Burroughs: Well, the General ordered him to gallop through the front lines with a message. Paralysed with funk. Couldn't move. General sent his adjutant, killed before he'd gone fifty yards. Sent his ADC – head blown off. Then he went through with the message himself – lost his arm, ruined his cricket.

Other 'names' associated with Hollywood Cricket Club at various times have been R C Sherriff, Anthony Bushell, Henry Stephenson, Ernest Torrance, Clive Brook, Basil Rathbone, Arthur Wimperis and Douglas Fairbanks, Jnr.; also Gilchrist Stuart and George Coulouris, who was not the first thespian to have an ambition in which he managed a travelling theatrical troupe that could double as a cricket team.

Aubrey Smith organized a number of games during the World War II years – he was nearly 80 – in aid of the British Services. Manning the 'public address', distributing programmes and making the tea involved some extremely attractive helpers: Greer Garson, Olivia de Havilland, Yvonne de Carlo, Gladys Cooper, Benita Hume, Evelyn Laye and Merle Oberon. A very young Elizabeth Taylor put in an appearance at one of these matches.

There are several stories surrounding Aubrey Smith and his attitude to cricket. On one occasion the only man available and willing to make up the side was William Boyd, creator of Hopalong Cassidy, ten-gallon hat, top boots, cowboy's pony and all. Hopalong had not the faintest notion of how to play cricket and therefore handled his bat in baseball fashion, rather like a policeman's truncheon. He had arrived at the ground fairly unobtrusively; Smith had been busy winning the toss and deciding to bat and nobody had especially noticed the fact that there was a substitute, let alone who it was.

Only when the seventh wicket fell and Hopalong ambled lackadaisically to the centre, six foot three of scrawn, dusty flannels and spurs poking alarmingly through the bottom of his pads, did reality strike home. The umpire enquired if he would like a guard. 'Start pitchin',' yelled Hopalong and then defiantly blew a balloon with the gum he had been chewing so energetically.

The first ball he missed easily; the second not quite so easily; the third, a slow full toss on the leg-side, was dispatched towards heaven with a velocity which gave the ball a chance of landing on the top of a skyscraper if only one had been close enough. Hopalong reacted as if galvanized. He scampered off wildly on a circular tour, from point to cover to mid-off to mid-on to square-leg and a final dash helter-skelter plummeting arms akimbo into his own wicket. A deafening quiet awaited the *coup de grace*. 'Well, I declare,' exclaimed the amazed Smith. He did not, of course.

BIBLIOGRAPHY

A multitude of sources have been combed; too many to itemize separately. The following have been important points of reference:

Newspapers, mainly *The Times* and *The Guardian*, 19th century onwards. Others are mentioned at the point in the text.
19th and 20th century magazines.
Wisden's Cricketers Almanack.
John Wisden's *Cricketers Notebooks.*
Wisden Cricket Monthly.
The Cricketer.
The Cricketer Book of Cricket Eccentrics – Martin-Jenkins.
The Cricketer Book of Cricket Disasters – Martin-Jenkins.
Who's Who of Cricketers – Bailey, Thorn, Wynne-Thomas.
Cricket: A History of its Growth and Development – Bowen.
Maiden Over – Nancy Joy.
Cricket: an heroic poem – James Love, edited Ashley-Cooper.
Great Sporting Eccentrics – Randall.
Bat, Ball, Wicket and all – Martineau.
All Round the Wicket – Brodribb.
Guiness Facts and Feats – Frindall.
Australian Cricket, the Game and the Players – Pollard.
The Hambledon Men – Lucas.
Cricket in the Writings of James Joyce – Whitelock.
Pageant of Cricket – Frith.
Journal of the Cricket Society.
Young Cricketers Tutor and Cricketers of My Time – Nyren.
The Way to Lords – Williams.